CONCEPTUAL PLANNING FOR
CREATIVE
LEARNING

Bruce M. Mitchell
Arnold F. Stueckle
Robert F. Wilkens

Eastern Washington State College
Cheney, Washington

KENDALL/HUNT PUBLISHING COMPANY
DUBUQUE, IOWA

CONTENTS

PREFACE

Not so many years ago, a young elementary school teacher faced his first group of bright young moppets. He was an eager young man who had listened carefully to the education professors during his course work. Now, he was anxious to put into practice some of the pedagogical precepts he had learned.

One thing all the professors had stressed repeatedly was the importance of rapport. And one sunny day, he found himself faced with a dilemma. While standing in the cafeteria line, one of the more precocious young ladies in his class approached him.

"Mr. Green, some of the kids wanted me to ask you something." Green turned and looked at the young lady who had suddenly diverted his attention from the pangs of hunger which were now quite prevalent.

"Yes, Susie, what is it?"

Clearing her throat ever so slightly, Susie replied: "They—they wanted to know if our class could watch the World Series tomorrow."

Green pondered the question carefully. None of his professors had ever mentioned this kind of request. They had talked about rapport, individual differences and creativity. These things were certainly important. He remembered how they said that in order to foster creativity, teachers had to be flexible. And what a way to establish rapport!

"I'll even bring my portable television set to school," Susie added, interrupting his decision-making process.

After smiling pleasantly and uttering the usual "We'll see," Green pondered the proposal further. Finally after considering all the factors involved, he decided to honor the young lady's request.

The next day the Series began and Green's class watched diligently. The students were delighted, and Green had undoubtedly enhanced his image with the group. His professors would be proud. The class watched the first two games with avid interest. At the conclusion of the second game, Mr. Green reminded his students that tonight was Open House. His very first.

The task at hand for this particular Open House was to present the parents with an overview of the year's program. Green was a trifle uneasy as they filed in dutifully and took seats in their youngsters' desks. The formal part went quite well. His opening joke was received with laughter and the parents listened intently. Then, Green called for questions. At first, no hands were raised. Then, he noticed Mrs. Dogood's hand at the rear of the room.

"I would like to know, Mr. Green, how you can justify spending two solid hours watching the World Series when my daughter still doesn't know how to multiply correctly?"

Green went into a state of shock. He muttered something about "our national pasttime" and "cultural heritage" while frantically searching for help, any kind of help. Fortunately for him, it came. Mrs. Brown said, "I'm grateful that my daughter had the opportunity to watch the Series. She hasn't been interested in anything before this."

"Me too," said Mr. Able. "I want my kid to like sports. Green is the first teacher who ever did anything like this before. I think it's great."

But Mrs. Dogood was not to be deterred that easily. "Yes," she argued, "I think it's important too, but why for two hours? If you made a math lesson out of it, the time would have been well spent."

Green raced home after the Open House and planned feverishly until 2:00 in the morning. On the next World Series day, working individually and in small groups, some students computed batting averages, kept score, figured out fielding percentages, slugging averages, and participated in all the other statistical activities connected with the game of baseball. Others did research on Abner Doubleday's contributions. Students wrote biographies about their favorite players and even did punning exercises. One committee painted a mural depicting baseball scenes. One boy even made a dictionary of baseball terminology. Another group of students dissected a "dead" baseball and a modern "lively" one and compared the differences.

The classroom teacher who is seriously committed to emerging concepts of instructional strategies is faced with a rather awesome challenge. Classroom practitioners and others sophisticated in areas of child growth and development recognize that youngsters bring with them a rather overwhelming variety of personalities and social backgrounds which have serious implications concerning the fruition of their intellectual capabilities.

Researchers have often stated that their findings show the impossibility of meaningful learning occurring without adequate motivation, a realization of purposes, and significant changes in student behavior.

Teacher Green was guilty of a common failing. Too often, lessons are undertaken without adequate planning. If you share some of the frustrations of Green and would like to acquire additional expertise in educational planning you may benefit from reading our book.

The remainder of the book consists of two parts plus appendices. Part One deals with long-range planning. Here, an attempt will be made to acquaint you with developing purposes of instruction, developing learning concepts, and deriving behavioral objectives.

Part Two will embody the topics listed above as they relate to daily planning. Specific examples will be given concerning daily objectives, activities, timing and organization, materials, and evaluation.

The appendices consist of seven sample units illustrating the topics discussed in the first two parts.

PART ONE

LONG-RANGE PLANNING

INTRODUCTION

Consider for a moment the professional activities of one of America's most successful college football coaches. Let's call him Ken McCool. When McCool prepares for a game, he and his entire staff consider every possible factor pertaining to the game of football. Such items as the crowd emotion, physical characteristics of the stadium, and players tipping off their play patterns, are some of the more subtle items which come under careful scrutiny. In addition, offensive and defensive strategies are studied over and over. A "game plan" or "playing style" is developed for each opponent.

When blessed with a runner like the one we are about to describe the strategy is simple. Let's name our fictitious all-American, Seth Streaker. Now, Seth stands about 6'3" tall, runs the hundred yard dash in 9.3 seconds, weighs about 210 pounds, has all the necessary moves, and is as tough as they come. In short, he's a once in a lifetime player. In a situation like this Coach McCool's strategy is simple. Give the ball to Seth and stand back. For one particular game, McCool and his staff met to plan game strategy. They decided to stay with their successful tactics since they were undefeated and were number one in the nation. Seth would carry the ball about forty times as usual.

However, the enemy coaches had also done their homework. They knew they would have to find a way to stop Seth. They decided to have their defensive roverback cover the outside of the field in order to cut down Seth's running room. In order to do this, they had to restrict their defensive coverage of the tight end. But Coach McCool's team seldom threw him a pass anyhow. They just let Streaker run—and run—and run.

For one half these defensive tactics worked beautifully. Coach McCool's carefully contrived game plan was not working. His team was in danger of losing its number one rating. However, McCool and his staff soon saw what was happening. They scrapped the game plan

1

and started passing to the tight end. The defensive roverback always had to take a couple of steps toward Seth because the quarterback kept faking the ball to him. This allowed the tight end to get free. After catching several key passes, McCool's team scored a touchdown. Now the roverback had to start watching the tight end. And soon the quarterback really did give the ball to Seth. It resulted in a 78 yard touchdown run and a win for McCool and his team. Because he changed his plans at the right time he got the win and maintained his team's number one ranking.

Thus, we have seen two things happen. First, in order to succeed in a venture, one must be well planned. Second, these carefully conceived plans must be discarded, altered, or augmented when necessary.

If you need more convincing, consider the heart surgeon who carefully plans to repair a damaged aorta through surgery. When making the necessary incisions, it is learned that a problem also exists in the bicuspid valve. The plans, so carefully plotted, are quickly changed.

The crucial question should now be clarified through these two analogies. Are we willing to operate in such a fashion in our profession? Can we derive such carefully conceived plans? Are we flexible enough to deviate from these plans when necessary?

In the two examples cited, it is important to note that the coach and the surgeon both were aware of their procedures. Their objectives were clear. Coach McCool's objective was to put more points on the scoreboard than his opponents. The objective of the heart surgeon was to repair the mechanism so it would pump blood in the proper manner. Both objectives were realized.

It then follows that if we are to achieve success in education, we must be able to state objectives clearly and evaluate them accurately. In order to accomplish this, we must know how to translate conceptual understandings into behavioral objectives. At the conclusion of a lesson or unit, we need some means of determining whether the student understands the concept. Thus, we must be able to actually see the student perform or observe the finished product in order to determine if these objectives have been attained.

Dr. Robert Mager suggests that an explicit teaching objective has three characteristics: (1) it identifies the terminal performance which the instruction tried to produce; (2) it describes the important conditions under which this performance should occur; and (3) it describes the standard of acceptable performance. Mager goes on to state that these three characteristics are not necessary in every objective, but may be used as guides to help a teacher know whether or not the objective is clear.*

The subject areas dealt with in the book have been divided into two sections. Part One deals with long range planning. Here, an attempt will be made to acquaint you with establishing purposes of instruction, developing learning concepts, and deriving behavioral objectives. Chapter three develops the Fourteen Basic Elements of Creative Behavior and shows how they can be integrated into the total planning process.

Part Two will embody the topics listed above as they relate to daily planning. Specific examples will be given concerning daily objectives, elements of creative behavior, activities, timing and organization, materials, and evaluation.

The appendices consist of sample units illustrating how lessons can be developed through the use of conceptual planning with behavioral objectives. Some of these samples illustrate ways in which the Fourteen Basic Elements can be incorporated into instructional planning.

A word of clarification is in order at this point. Some educators continue to express concern about the possibility of specific objectives creating an over-emphasis on learning subject matter and fostering undue conformity. Consequently, our book will concentrate on planning techniques which will nurture processes such as: developing the ability to improve divergent thinking skills; enhancing creative problem-solving skills; increasing environmental awareness; improving the self-image; and becoming sensitive to the needs of mankind.

It seems logical that these and other similar processes could be developed more effectively through careful planning rather than merely being left to chance or happenstance.

---

*Robert F. Mager, *Preparing Instructional Objectives* (Palo Alto, California: Fearon Publishers, 1962), p. 12.

CONCEPTUAL LESSON PLANNING MODEL

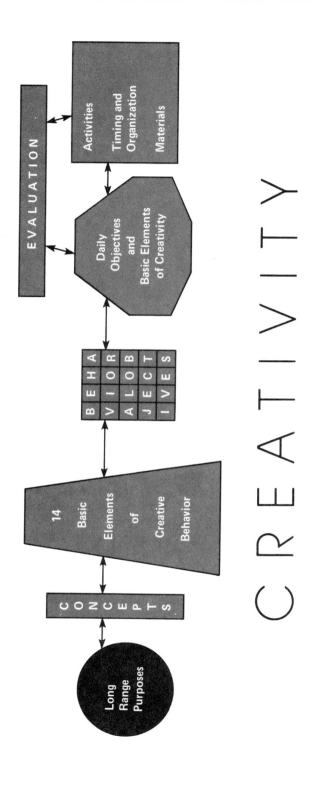

CHAPTER ONE

LONG-RANGE PURPOSES

Let us reconsider the saga of coach McCool and his team. Earlier we discussed the game plan which McCool and his staff devised to defeat their current foe. However, this single game plan actually constituted only a part of a long-range purpose which McCool had in mind. This long-range purpose was to remain number one in the nation. In order to retain this ranking it was necessary to recruit appropriate material, plan and conduct purposeful practice sessions, scout opponents carefully, and use the talents of players to their fullest extent. The classroom teacher must utilize a similar plan.

The first task in educational planning is in identifying long-range purposes. We must know what we are attempting to do. Long-range purposes should clearly define achievements that are to be realized after the learner has been involved in certain activities. An important process in the realization of these achievements is the selection of appropriate activities. Unless long-range purposes are identified at the outset of planning sequences, the selected activities tend to become an end in themselves, and have limited value. Long-range purposes also provide the teacher with a system of checks and balances which offer an appropriate variety of activities. Without these purposes, many lessons tend to become little more than drill and memorization. Also, during the planning sequence of the long-range purposes, the teacher must contantly gear instructional plans to the individual characteristics of the students.

The Conceptual Lesson Planning Model which first appears on page 4 provides a visual picture of the steps involved in the long range-daily planning processes. The model will be used throughout the book in order to portray the steps involved as they are discussed in the narrative. It should be noted that the arrows run both ways which indicates that in the evaluation processes it is necessary to re-trace the steps involved in the planning sequences.

A typical fifth grade social studies curriculum guide might include the following areas of study: (1) the discovery and exploration of the United States; (2) the colonial period; and (3) the westward movement. In the planning sequence a teacher might include the following long-range purposes pertaining to example number one above: to know who the early discoverers and explorers were and to determine the reasons for their exploits. The long-range purposes for the colonial period could consist of: understanding the background of the colonists and developing an awareness of the problems in colonial life. Two long-range purposes for the westward movement might be: knowing about the types of early transportation and understanding the problems the pioneers faced in providing for their basic needs.

There are, naturally, many other examples of long-range purposes that could and should be used. However, it is hoped that the examples cited illustrate that long-range purposes should be established as a point of origin. In later chapters it will be shown that long-range purposes must be determined prior to establishing conceptual understandings, deriving behavioral objectives, and the evaluation process.

It should be emphasized that the long-range purposes may be stated in non-behavioral terms. A mere statement of goals written in a rather general manner will suffice.

Summary

Many people have stated that they were successful because they had a purpose. This statement holds true for teachers as well as people in other fields. A teacher must do some careful planning before engaging in any teaching. The first step in this planning should be spent in identifying long-range purposes. Then the teacher should begin to do more specific planning. This should include developing conceptual understandings, deriving behavioral objectives, enhancing creative problem-solving skills, and evaluation. However, it is important to remember that the long-range purposes for the lesson need not always be written behaviorally.

Notes

CONCEPTUAL LESSON PLANNING MODEL

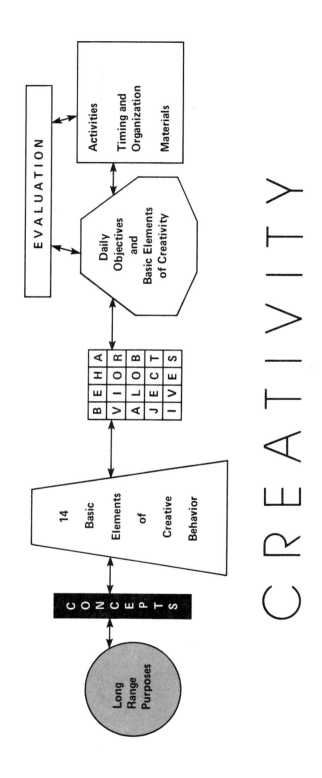

CREATIVITY

CHAPTER TWO

DEVELOPING LEARNING CONCEPTS

Mrs. Smart, an inexperienced third grade teacher, was attempting to teach her class the concept that national forests are used for their timber as well as for recreational purposes. After talking to the students for about twenty minutes she noticed that Bill had a puzzled look on his face.

"What don't you understand?" she asked.

"I think I know what national forests are," said Bill, "but why do baseball players in the National League have to play in national forests?"

Before Mrs. Smart could answer, Jane said, "I don't know the answer to Bill's question, but I do know that if trees aren't cut carefully the forests will be 'wrecked' places for people to see."

Mrs. Smart failed to realize that being able to verbalize a mass of words that have little or no real meaning is not necessarily learning. Students can learn only to the extent that their previous experience will permit. Evidently the only understanding Bill had of the word "national" was in association with baseball. He did not know the difference between national forests and other types of forests. Jane probably wasn't listening too well, or perhaps Mrs. Smart was talking too much, and so Jane had the words "recreation" and "wreck" confused. It is quite apparent that one of the causes of Jane's and Bill's confusion was that they did not have the knowledge to understand the concept. Therefore, Mrs. Smart had not adequately prepared the students before the concept was presented. Students acquire conceptual understandings outside of school and from a broad base of experiences that can be organized by skillful teachers. This places a heavy responsibility on the teacher since there is no magic formula to tell him the degree of readiness of a particular student for learning a given concept. This information can be obtained through careful observation of students and by preparing them for the new concept to be introduced. Simply stated we can say that learning must start with the knowledge the student has brought into the classroom.

In Chapter One it was mentioned that a typical fifth grade social studies curriculum might include the westward movement as an area of study. To develop some of the concepts necessary for understanding the westward movement it is important to provide students with the opportunity to express their ideas about this period of history. To some students the movement westward was the gold rush in California; to others it was the covered wagon pulled by oxen; and some students, especially boys, immediately think of cowboys and Indians. Teachers, in evaluating these ideas, should do so in terms of the students' experiences rather than their own. These ideas, added to those expressed by other students, provide the teacher with the opportunity to extend and refine the students' concepts of the westward movement.

Teachers often fail to realize that by inhibiting the free expression of students they might be obstructing the learning process. Some teachers who allow students to express themselves often place too much emphasis on what is *wrong* with the student's concept. These same teachers, and others, sometimes ridicule and humiliate students for a misconception. Misconceptions and failure can become vehicles for creative development. In some instances a student may even be forcefully punished for expressing an erroneous concept. A student, experiencing this type of teacher reaction, may become taciturn and disinterested in learning. Teachers should allow students to express ideas fully and view these ideas from a positive rather than a negative point of view. Misconceptions, if known, can be corrected through proper classroom instruction.

Ragan stated that the following principles of learning are often not utilized: (1) *Learning should be affiliated with student purposes if it is to be effective.* This should not imply that a teacher must use only student purposes. He or she should expand these purposes and create situations which develop others which are necessary. (2) *Growth and learning are continuous.* A child has learned many things before starting to attend school. Even after entering school many things from out-of-school experiences are learned. It is the responsibility of the school and teacher to fuse these learnings. (3) *There are individual differences among students.* This principle has been known for many years and has been discussed frequently; however, until recently, not much was done about it. Later, the subject of meeting these individual differences will be dealt with quite extensively. (4) *Students experience concomitant learnings.* Incidental learning often takes place during a learning experience and may be as important or more important to the student than the planned learning outcome. (5) *Learning should be adjusted to the maturity of the student.* The principles of readiness and individual differences are closely allied with maturity. Also, maturity should not be confused with chronological age. Many school districts are finally realizing that all five-year-olds are not ready to enter kindergarten! (6) *Students learn best by participation in actual or vicarious experiences.* This principle has also been known for many years and, yet, many teachers do not apply it in their teaching.* It is true that due to the lack of facilities, equipment, etc., these principles are often difficult to implement. However, teachers should constantly be aware of these principles and employ them more readily. The principles cited above are certainly not complete but it is hoped that these examples will remind you that learning experiences should be planned with the students as the focal point.

After the preliminary tasks of the teacher and students have been completed the concept is ready to be introduced. Since one presentation is sometimes not sufficient, strategies used in teaching the concepts should be reviewed and supplemented. In this way the students will be discovering the concepts through various experiences.

If you recall, in Chapter One, it was stated that long-range purposes should be established as a point of origin and must be determined prior to developing conceptual understandings. In this same chapter, two examples of long-range purposes were given. These were in conjunction with the westward movement and were "knowing about the types of early transportation" and "understanding the problems pioneers faced in providing for their basic needs." By using the suggested student activities in Table 1-1 some of the concepts developed by the teacher and students for these two purposes might be achieved. (A later chapter explains in detail how student activities are implemented in daily planning.)

Table 1-1 is not complete and the placement of the student activities may be rearranged according to the teacher's individual wishes. As was stated earlier, previous presentations should be reviewed and supplemented. (See Table 1-1)

The students, both during and after the learning experience, should feel that it was enjoyable and that they have learned something worthwhile. The students and teacher should also have learned more about themselves because of the contributions they made during the learning experience. These attitudes can be used by the teacher as a valuable evaluative tool. However, evaluation should also

*William B. Ragan, *Modern Elementary Curriculum.* (New York: Holt, Rinehart, and Winston, Inc., 1961), pp. 49-52.

TABLE 1
Suggested Student Activities for Teaching Concepts

Concepts	Suggested Student Activities
(1) During a period in our history many people moved westward	Discussion—reasons for westward movement; ethnic groups Films and filmstrips Time chart Map work to show routes followed
(2) Different types of land transportation were used	Library research—reports Scroll theater Bulletin board displays Models Gather and display still pictures Flip charts
(3) While on the trail people had to provide for their basic needs	Field trip to museum Dioramas Display table Short dramatizations Paper and pencil test
(4) The early pioneers moved westward	Prepare and give dramatic play—script, direction, costumes, etc. done by students with guidance of teacher Review of play Paper and pencil test

be based on behavioral objectives. These two topics, deriving behavioral objectives and evaluation, are discussed in later chapters.

Many educators entertain varying notions about the composition of a concept. Some learning theorists consider one word such as "democracy" to be a concept. However, for purposes of this planning process the authors have chosen to think of a concept in terms of the samples as stated on Table 1-1. Thus, examples included in the appendices will be stated in this fashion.

The model used in this book for explaining concepts will consist of three steps. The data are merely the facts and information which are *collected* and *processed* to form the *concepts*. The concept will be expressed in sentences which denote an idea. Formulation of the concept requires certain kinds of pertinent data.

Summary

Briefly, let us review what has been discussed in this chapter. Teachers should preassess the intellectual attainments of their students before introducing a new concept. This information can be obtained by careful observation, letting students express their ideas freely, and through the use of various data gathering devices. After the teacher has acquired this information he should use it to help prepare the students for the introduction of the concept. The teacher must be very observant and develop a classroom atmosphere that is free from ridicule, unnecessary punishment, and other inhibiting forces.

After using various activities in order to teach the concepts deemed important, it may be necessary to review the strategies used and try new ones when the concepts are not understood. It is important that the classroom teachers use other student activities at this point.

For purposes of this book a three-step conceptual model will be used. Data is the necessary information which must be processed in order to arrive at a conceptual understanding. The concept will be considered a sentence which describes an idea. In this context, the concept will not be identified by just one word.

CONCEPTUAL LESSON PLANNING MODEL

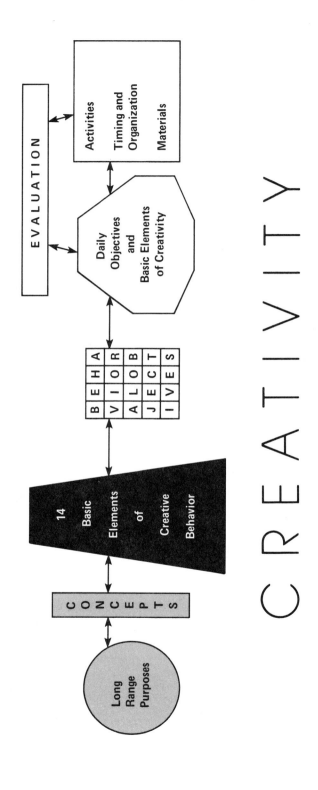

CHAPTER THREE

PLANNING FOR CREATIVE PROBLEM SOLVING

Before proceeding further through the conceptual planning model it is necessary to focus attention on another topic crucial in the total educational process. The subject of creativity is a rather new one since most of the research conducted has been undertaken since 1950. Little attention is paid to creative thinking in the educational environment and studies show that most attention is focused on rote memorization and the acquisition of lower levels of knowledge.

One useful definition of creativity has been developed by Guilford who has generated the notion of divergent thinking. Divergent thinking involves the production of many answers or solutions from a single idea. Creativity includes the principles of divergent thinking which help generate fluency, flexibility, originality, and elaboration. Thus, creativity refers to the ideas which are unique to the individual who generated them.*

While there are numerous reasons for the development of creative thinking processes in the classroom, a couple of rather obvious reasons should suffice here. We are all aware that the world is facing several enviromental crises. Our population is increasing so rapidly that major famines threaten humanity. We are using oxygen more rapidly than we are able to replace it. The world's oil supply is becoming depleted and half of our kindergarteners will be employed in occupations which don't exist today. The rather obvious conclusion is that we desperately will need the creative talents of all of tomorrow's citizens if we are to survive.**

Further testimony to the need for developing creative behavior more fully is provided by Calvin Taylor who said: "The development of fully functioning individuals has long been an avowed objective of

---

*Guilford, J.P. *The Nature of Human Intelligence.* (New York: McGraw-Hill, 1967), p. 138.
**Mitchell, Bruce and Wilkens, Robert. "Creative Problem Solving: A Crucial Tool for Dealing with Tomorrow's World," *Illinois School Journal,* Vol. 54 (Spring-Summer, 1974), pp. 25-32.

education. We believe that education in a democracy should help all individuals develop their talents fully—to become as near self-actualized as possible. To fully develop the intellectual capacities of our children and to lead them closer to self-actualization, the abilities involved in developing creative thinking and creativity cannot be ignored. The traditional measures of intelligence assess only a few of man's intellectual talents. Man's complex mental operations are not being fully developed or assessed. Among them is his ability to think and act creatively."*

Although our society needs creative geniuses, our focus is *not* on trying to develop each student in such a fashion. While this might be a worthy aim, the literature suggests that such a goal is totally unattainable. However, we do know that where the development of creative problem-solving skills is a primary goal, it is possible to significantly raise the creativity scores of students.** Hence, we feel it is imperative to leave the reader with some substantive means of developing creativity in the total classroom approach. It is evident that this development does not occur by chance or happenstance.

The conceptual planning model which has been developed in this book provides the teacher with a usable instrument for creating plans in any of the curricular areas. The samples in the appendix deal with a variety of subjects.

So far, we have described briefly the nature of the creative process and the necessity for developing each student's creative thinking skills. Studies show the creative potential of students can be increased if teachers plan for it consciously. Let us now turn to more specific classroom strategies for developing creative behavior.

Through an analysis of the research and our own experiences in the field, *Fourteen Basic Elements of Creative Behavior* have been identified. Much of the early work was done by Newton Metfessel of the University of Southern California. Through his work in creative problem solving, he identified *Twenty-Six Correlates of Creative Be-*

---

*Taylor, Calvin in *Igniting Creative Potential* II by Beverly C. Lloyd, JoAnn B. Seghini, and Gilbert Stevenson. (Sandy, Utah: Jordon School District, 1974), pp. iv, v.
**Mitchell, Bruce. "The Classroom Pursuit of Creativity: One Strategy that Worked," *Journal of Research and Development in Education,* Vol. 4, #3. Spring, 1971. pp. 57-61.

havior* which were crucial ingredients of the creative process. Many of our ideas stem from his excellent list. However, these have been synthesized somewhat and other key ingredients have been added. Thus, *The Fourteen Basic Elements of Creative Behavior* were created and are discussed later in the chapter. As with any such list, the reader will notice some overlapping among the various principles and classroom activities given. However, the fourteen elements identified herein have important characteristics which require their inclusion. It would appear that teachers who consciously attempt to utilize these principles will have more success in increasing the creative development of their students.

In using the fourteen basic elements, the teacher must first select the appropriate curricular area to be considered. While secondary teachers normally deal with their teaching disciplines, elementary level practitioners are blessed with a wide variety of curricular areas from which to choose! Next, the teacher must study the list of elements and decide which seem to be the most germane to the curricular topic under consideration. It will be seen that each of the fourteen elements identifies sample classroom activities which are useful in the development of that item. Many teachers will be able to think of other activities to supplement the list.

Then, when writing the plans, the elements which are to be utilized should be identified as part of the long-range purposes in order to know at the outset the goals for creativity development. Next, the elements are also included with the daily objectives. It is vital that the elements should be chosen at the *outset* of the planning process. If the teacher merely writes a plan in one of several curricular areas and casually tacks on a principle or two without planning appropriate activities, it is highly unlikely that any creativity will occur.

It is crucial that the use of the fourteen basic elements be used regularly in the planning process if the creative potential of students is to emerge. It is also imperative that the elements be dealt with regularly in planning instructional sequences. For example, if the teacher provided many opportunities for brainstorming, but neglected originality, only one portion of the creative process would be developed.

*Metfessel, Newton S., "Twenty-Six Correlates of Creative Behavior, with Examples of Classroom Processes Towards their Development," Unpublished paper, University of Southern California, 1965.

The following list, then, should be considered carefully when planning for the development of creative behavior through the use of the conceptual planning model.

The Fourteen Basic Elements of Creative Behavior

1. Development of Humor
2. Fluency
3. Flexibility
4. Originality
5. Elaboration
6. Self-concept
7. Experimenting with and Testing Ideas and Hunches
8. Learning from Failure
9. Tolerance for Ambiguity
10. Resourcefulness
11. Problem Sensitivity
12. Synergy
13. Imagination
14. Synectics

Obviously, models of this nature are never completely unique. We have chosen what we feel are the most crucial elements from various sources, and have added others which we deem important.

The model includes a description of each element and offers suggestions for classroom activities aiding in its development.

I. Development of Humor

   A.   Summary: The literature suggests that humor is a crucial ingredient of the creative personality. Thus, the emphasis should be on helping people to become better producers and consumers of humor.

   B.   Classroom Practices.

         1.   Activities which reward the creation of humorous ideas.

               a.   Development of the ability to pun and to enjoy punning.

               b.   Creation of humorous stories, limerics, poems, etc.

           c.   Activities involving humorous art work such as cartoons or droodles.

II. Fluency

    A.   Summary: Referring to the ability to create many responses to a given stimulus; the concept of fluency can be thought of in terms of "odds." If a larger number of responses can be generated, the odds are greater that a creative solution can be reached.

    B.   Classroom Practices.

        1.   Activities which aid in increasing idea development.

            a.   Listing objects in a special way (round, rough, sharp, square, etc.).

            b.   Brainstorming: list of possible solutions to a given problem.

            c.   Tasks requiring students to invent new descriptive words.

III. Flexibility

    A.   Summary: Flexibility in the *Torrance Tests of Creative Thinking* refers to the ability to produce a variety of ideas that may cause a shift from one thought pattern or category to another.

    B.   Classroom Practices.

        1.   Tasks in which the instructions given should encourage the solicitation of as many different kinds of responses as possible.

            a.   Asking "open ended" questions. For example: "What are all the characteristics of a wooden-handled hammer?" (Typical responses might be: steel head, wooden handle, operated by hand, round head, oval handle, attached by the wedge principle, steel forged, shellaced handle, etc. These responses fall into various categories such as shape, materials, method of attachment, etc.)

        b.   Unusual uses tasks. (i.e., "How many uses can you think of for a brick, tin can, wrecked car, etc.")

        c.   Tasks that focus on comparing the differences between two items. By encouraging the students to identify as many different kinds of differences as possible, and placing the responses into categories such as religion, climate, customs, language, etc.

IV. Originality

A.   Summary: Most researchers feel that originality is one of the basic ingredients of the creative process. The term refers simply to the uniqueness or rarity of a response. The idea produced would be unusual, clever, even "outlandish." There are two kinds of originality which should be considered, however, according to most creativity researchers. First, the response which is original in the life span of the individual, and second, the response which is original for a total environment.

B.   Classroom Practices.

    1.   Original ideas should be encouraged and be rewarded.

        a.   Brainstorming activities which encourage suspending judgment in order to generate unique responses.

        b.   Encouraging the use of original humor.

        c.   The use of similes and metaphors to compare things that are similar and different, and to describe objects more vividly.

        d.   Providing opportunities for aesthetic expression. (i.e., Writing about a winter scene.)

V. Elaboration

A.   Summary: Generally, this element refers to the capacity to develop a chain of ideas based on the embellishment of an original notion.

B.   Classroom Practices.
   1.   Activities in general which provide a stimulus and require the students to develop responses which build on one another. (A chaining effect.)
      a.   Solving problems with given conditions and items which allow for sequential developments leading to ultimate solutions. (Rube Goldberg exercise.)
      b.   Artistic activities which allow the students to create pictures or designs from simple "squiggle" lines.
      c.   Invention of new games and/or rules in physical education, based on a well-known game.
      d.   Writing endings to unfinished stories.

VI. Self-concept

A.   Summary: This element deals with the development of the self-assessment mechanism. It has been suggested by some behavioral scientists that praise should be internal rather than external. Therefore, minimal use of such external praise devices as the "gold star," "the good work corner," and the like is suggested.

B.   Classroom Practices.
   1.   Activities that require students to describe their product or performance in terms of its strengths, its weaknesses, and possible means of improvement.
      a.   Art projects such as drawings, murals, dioramas, etc.
      b.   Assessment of physical education skills. (i.e., Serve in tennis, the "bump" in volleyball, fielding in softball, etc.)
      c.   Individualized instruction programs which require the student to plot his or her own progress in terms of improvement.

VII. Experimenting with and Testing Ideas and Hunches

A.   Summary: This element relates to the creative problem-solving process developed by S.J. Parnes. This five-stage

process consists of: (1) fact-finding; (2) problem-finding; (3) idea-finding; (4) solution-finding; and (5) acceptance-finding.*

B.   Classroom Practices.

    1.   Students need to utilize available facts and/or information before engaging in the latter part of the process. Ample time should be allowed for students to play around with ideas and hunches.

        a.   Use of "What Would Happen If" questions such as—"What would happen if the polar ice caps melted, raising the level of the oceans by ten feet?"

        b.   Science activities using the scientific method (hypothesizing, observing, and evaluating the findings in terms of the original hypothesis).

VIII.   Learning From Failure

A.   Summary: Much of the literature has dealt with the elimination of failure from the school environment. However, perhaps of more importance is the development of an atmosphere in which failure is permissible. The literature indicates that one element of creative problem solving is in learning from the failing situation.

B.   Classroom Practices.

    1.   Establishment of an environment which says: "Go ahead and try something. If it doesn't work, let's find out why."

        a.   Reading of the failures of such successful people as the Curies, Verner von Braun, Churchill, Edison, and others.

        b.   Encouraging students to attempt tasks where failure is possible. (i.e., Discovery method in science, social studies, mathematics, or other curricular areas.)

---

*Parnes, S.J. *Creative Behavior Guidebook.* (New York: Charles Scribner's Sons, 1967), pp. 184-185.

IX. Tolerance for Ambiguity

    A.   Summary: Metfessel describes this element as: "Feeling comfortable when faced by a complex social issue having opposed principles intermingled, as deviation from a standard or acceptance of a state of affairs capable of alternative outcomes."*

    B.   Classroom Practices.

        1.   Helping students to accept the fact that not all questions are totally right or totally wrong, and that there are "gray" areas which must sometimes be tolerated.

            a.   Utilization of inquiry techniques of discussion developed by Richard Suchman.

            b.   Utilization of Higher Level Thinking Skills developed by Hilda Taba.

            c.   Rewarding students who help thwart the premature closure of a discussion.

            d.   Encouraging of different or unique questions and responses. (i.e., Flowers "feel" nice rather than flowers smell nice.)

X. Resourcefulness

    A.   Summary: Metfessel describes this element as "An aggregate of one's available property as skills, judgment, capacity for finding or adjusting means, power of achievement."**

    B.   Classroom Practices.

        1.   Students, at times, plan their own learning activities that could have accidentally stemmed from a simple discussion. This could result in long-range tasks which require student performance over an extended period of time.

            a.   Creation of a weather station including a barometer, hygrometer, thermometer, and

*Metfessel, Newton. "Twenty-Six Correlates of Creative Behavior," Unpublished paper, University of Southern California, 1965, p. 3.

**Ibid.

           annemometer to analyze climatic conditions.

    b.   Use of the scientific method and scientific experimentation.

    c.   Physical education activities where students have to "make do" with substitute equipment. (i.e., Invent a game which requires the use of two volleyballs and two kickballs or one badminton racquet and one shuttlecock.)

    d.   Having students solve simulated problems. (i.e., The moon landing exercise where participants have fifteen items which they must rank order according to their importance.)

XI. Problem Sensitivity

    A.   Summary: It has been suggested by many educational practitioners that persons who have the capacity to recognize problems are more apt to work on them, and ultimately determine solutions.

    B.   Classroom Practices.

        1.   Encouraging students to identify problems and develop strategies for their solution. Videotaping of pupil participation in order to assist them in the problem-solving process.

            a.   Urging students to question answers as well as to answer questions.

            b.   Having students create hypothetical problems for which others could supply creative solutions.

            c.   Assist students in writing problem statements based on need assessments.

            d.   "How would you prevent dishonesty in governments—the Watergate scandals?"

XII. Synergy

    A.   Summary: "Behavior of integral aggregate systems unpredicted by behaviors of any of their components of subassemblies of their components."* When two or more elements are interacted in a unique manner, the result can be greater than any or all of its parts. For example, the Japanese-designed machine that turns garbage into odor-free and unbreakable construction blocks.**

B. Classroom Practices.

1. Relating accounts of synergetic problem solutions such as the Swedish trash disposal device for apartment dwellings. The smog-free incinerator creates the energy necessary for running the vacuum system which clears the "trash duct system" to which each apartment is connected.

   a. Creating collages in art activities.

   b. Creating useful objects out of scrap. (i.e., A New York man constructs clothing out of soft drink pull tabs.)

   c. Creating murals where the students all participate in the planning and actual construction.

   d. Utilization of product improvement exercises where students are asked to improve a given product, process, game, object, etc.

   e. Development of a classroom environment in which there are lots of "realia" which can be used and observed by the students.

XIII. Imagination

A. Summary: Albert Einstein has said that imagination is more important than knowledge. Imagination, of course, refers to the capacity of pretending, or engaging in fantasy-related thought processes.

B. Classroom Practices.

---

*Fuller, R.B. *No More Secondhand God.* (Carbondale, Illinois: Southern Illinois University Press, 1963), p. 130.
**Parnes, *loc. cit.*

1.   Developing a classroom environment and atmosphere which inspires the use of imagination.

   a.   Unusual uses exercises which concentrate on familiar objects. (i.e., Bottles, cups, gum wads, etc.)

   b.   Creative writing exercises. (i.e., Having students write the biggest lie they can think of.)

   c.   Brainstorming. (i.e., Because of the fuel shortage, the internal combustion engine is an endangered species. What alternative methods of transportation might be possible solutions to this problem?)

   d.   Story telling by both students and the teacher.

   e.   Supplying titles for plots or stories.

XIV. Synectics

A.   Summary: The term "synectics" is from the Greek and refers to the uniting of different and seemingly irrelevant elements. The rationale for using synectics in the creative problem-solving process has been that emotional components are more important than rational ones.

B.   Classroom Practices.

   1.   Providing opportunities for students to express their emotions in new and sometimes strange situations.

      a.   Playing with words, meanings, and definitions. (i.e., A calendar is like a mirror because: . . .)

      b.   Playing with scientific laws and concepts. (i.e., What would happen if there were no gravity?)

      c.   Use of the personal analogy. (i.e., Showing a picture of a fireman putting out a fire and asking "What animal looks like this?")

      d.   Use of the direct analogy. (i.e., Bell's invention of the telephone was based on his clinical knowledge of the human ear because of his work with the deaf.)

      e.   Use of the symbolic analogy. This involves the use of objective and impersonal images to describe problems. Groups can use these in terms of poetic responses.

      f.   Use of the fantasy analogy. Individuals or groups can create solutions which have a magical or fantasy quality. Then, they try to bring the solutions to a practical level.*

      g.   Use of feelings in a problem-solving situation. (i.e., What would it "feel like" to be that object. Pretend to be that object.)

Summary

It should be stressed that this chapter in *no way* constitutes an entire description of the creative process or the means by which it can be developed. At best, it is a brief introduction to the subject. Hopefully, the reader will consult the more detailed accounts of creativity by the authors listed as references in this chapter and other respected authorities. These individuals have toiled for years compiling data, writing, conducting workshops, and lecturing on the subject. By selective reading, individuals can gain important insights into such topics as the nature of the creative process, classroom environments which assist or impede the development of creativity, characteristics of creative people, character traits necessary for teachers and administrators involved in creativity projects, and the measurement of creativity.

However, this brief introduction, compiled with additional research and/or participation in inservice programs or college classes on creativity should enable the teacher to plan more effective programs. Hopefully, such programs will enrich the lives of students while increasing their potential to think and solve problems creatively.

*Adapted from: Torrance, E. Paul and Myers, R.E. *Creative Learning and Teaching.* (New York: Dodd, Mead and Company, 1971), pp. 91-92.

Finally, it would be appropriate to keep in mind a term attributable to Horace Walpole who created that fascinating account of the princes of Serendip who had the ability of making unexpected discoveries while looking for something else. The term, serendipity, refers to that unique capacity. The classroom teacher should strive to create an atmosphere which encourages serendipity. While the term has not been included as one of the Basic Elements of Creative Behavior, it permeates each of the fourteen. It refers to the accidental discovery, experimentation, the "discovery approach" to learning, and stresses the novel approach or the unique way of dealing with the environment.

Perhaps it can be described most succinctly by relating the story of the Pennsylvanian who built a campfire while hunting and noticed that an outcropping of rocks caught fire. The rocks turned out to be one of the first coal beds ever discovered in the United States. Thus, this term is critical to the total creative process and teachers should promote and nurture serendipitous behavior in the schoolroom and out.

Notes

CONCEPTUAL LESSON PLANNING MODEL

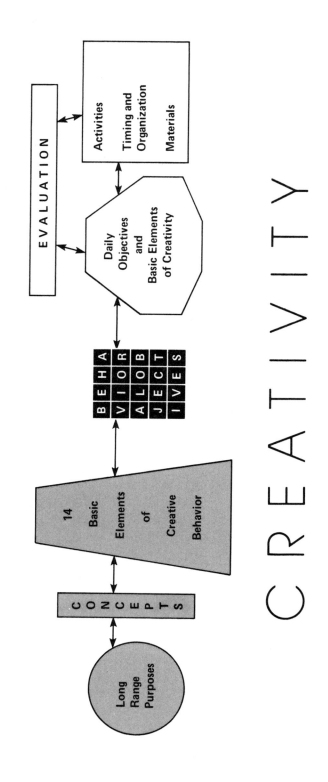

CHAPTER FOUR

DERIVING BEHAVIORAL OBJECTIVES

Mrs. Smart, our third grade teacher, has difficulty in stating her behavioral objectives. After reading the following exchange of notes see if you can understand why.

Feb. 15th

Dear Mrs. Smart,

I think the grade you gave Susan on her cursive writing test is very unfair. Three weeks ago when I asked you how I could help Susan improve her writing you said I should help her practice writing all the letters of the alphabet. You also stated that if she could write the letters neatly she would receive a good grade (probably an "A" or "B") on her test since you would base your grades on this objective. Susan has also told me that you told the other pupils to practice writing the letters of the alphabet so they could get a good grade. On Susan's test you commented that she did very well on writing the letters but that she couldn't name the strokes used in cursive writing. I had no idea she was to know the names of the various strokes. If you had graded the test on what you said you were going to, Susan would have received a much better grade than the "C" you gave her.

I will be anxiously awaiting your reply.

Mrs. Johnson

Feb. 15th

Dear Mrs. Johnson,

I was very sorry to hear that you were disappointed in Susan't test grade. I did tell you and the pupils that their test grade would be based on how well they could write the letters of the alphabet. However, we did spend ten minutes one day and five minutes another day on naming the various strokes used in writing so I wanted to see if the pupils had been paying attention. I believe students should know more about cursive writing than just being able to write well. If pupils are really learning they must know certain facts.

I do want you to know that Susan's writing has improved with the additional practice she has done at home.

Yours truly,

Mrs. Smart

Knowing something about behavioral objectives you immediately realized that Mrs. Smart fell into a common trap—that of stating certain behavioral objectives but then adding other objectives. Perhaps she also wanted some "trick questions" on her test so that students would really "think" and the test grades wouldn't be too high.

Some primary teachers may feel that knowing the various strokes in cursive writing is an important concept. The point is that if these are the teachers' feelings then they should focus on this concept, spend sufficient time developing the concept, and derive appropriate behavioral objectives which would measure its understanding. If the student cannot achieve the behavioral objectives the teacher may not have done a satisfactory job of stating the objectives and/or utilizing appropriate learning procedures.

A behavioral objective describes a desired behavior change in students who must demonstrate this change so you know they have achieved it. Thus, writers of behavioral objectives must *clearly* state what the student will be doing to show that the objective has been accomplished. Sounds simple? Okay, let's try an example: The student will understand how to add decimals. If you read this objective carefully you will notice there are many interpretations that can be made. Two of these are: (1) what is meant by the word "understand," and (2) what is meant by the word "decimals?" Does this objective clearly state what the student will be doing to show he or she has achieved the desired change? Obviously not. Therefore, it must be made more clear. Is this better? The student will be able to add decimals to the hundredths place. Yes, this is an improvement since it states what the student must do. However, do we know how well or how much he or she is to do? No. Let's try to clarify again. Given a twenty item test on adding decimals to the hundredths place the student must add correctly at least twelve problems within a twenty-five minute period of time. This statement describes the behavior, the lower limit of acceptable performance, and the conditions under which the student will demonstrate the desired change of behavior. In other words, it *clearly* states what the student will be doing to show the objective has been achieved.

At this point, you may be saying to yourself, "Why all the fuss over stating behavioral objectives? I already know what I want to teach." For the moment, let's assume this statement is valid and look at your teaching from the student's viewpoint. Is it clear to him what you are attempting to teach? If it isn't, perhaps you need to state your objectives more precisely in order to increase learning effectiveness. Now, let's return to the assumption concerned with knowing what to teach. Please spend five minutes reflecting on what you taught recently. Did you *really* know what to teach? Were the items you taught the most important or the most easily taught? Were they items you liked to teach because you knew a lot about them and felt safe teaching them? Did the students know what you were teaching? Did they have the ackground to understand it? Did you use the most effective tear ing techniques? Did the students do well on the tests you gave th n? These questions, plus many others, should indicate that clearl tated behavioral objectives are vital to teaching and learning.

In Part one of this book a reference was made to Mager. This reference stated that an objective has three characteristics: (1) it identifies the terminal performance of the students, (2) it describes the nportant conditions under which the performance will occur, nd (3) it describes the standard of acceptable performance. Mager also stated that these three characteristics are not necessary in every behavioral objective, but may be used as guides to help a teacher know whether or not the objective is clear.*

One of the common difficulties encountered by many people in writing behavioral objectives is the use of verbs such as understand, learn, comprehend, appreciate, enjoy, know, and others. Although these are fine terms for use in the statement of general goals, they do not indicate observable behavior. In order to measure the attainment of such conditions, it is necessary to state goals so they can be measured by observing behavior. Infinitives such as "to define," "to recall," "to translate," and "to prepare," are examples of terms which can be readily used to measure behavior.

The next step is to decide on the appropriate direct object which should be used with the infinitive in order to state measurable behavioral objectives. Consider the following: Given a pencil and paper the student will be able to list five effects of the Supreme Court Decision of 1954 pertaining to equality of the races. The infinitive (to list) and the object (effects) are clearly measurable by observing student behavior. Further, the three characteristics of behavioral objectives have been developed. The statement identifies the terminal performance of the student. The standards of acceptable performance (five) were stated. Also, the conditions under which the performance would occur (given a paper and pencil) was stated.

In order to increase teaching effectiveness, it is often desirable to determine the classes of behavior indicated in written objectives.

*Mager, *Preparing Instructional Objectives,* p. 12.

Educators have found that it is quite effective to consider a three category classification scheme. Thus, objectives are quite often referred to as falling into the congnitive, affective, or psychomotor domains. These categories refer to Bloom's use of the cognitive, affective, and psychomotor domains of behavior which are identified as follows:

1. *Cognitive Domain:* All behavior dealing with the recall or recognition of knowledge and the development of intellectual abilities and skills. The taxonomy divides the cognitive domain into six catagories which will be dealt with later.

2. *Affective Domain:* All behaviors that describe changes of interest, attitudes, and values, and the development of appreciation and adequate adjustment.

3. *Psychomotor Domain:* All behaviors that are primarily concerned with the performance of a physical activity.*

Without going into great detail, the six categories of the cognitive domain will be discussed briefly. Level one, or the *knowledge level,* merely involves the recall of specific information. It is sometimes referred to as the memory level. Most classroom questions are asked at this level of sophistication.

Level two, the *comprehension level,* represents the basic or lowest level of understanding. At this point, understandings of a simple nature are communicated; however, fullest implications are not yet derived.

Level three is the *application level.* Abstract ideas, theories, or principles can be used to solve problems. For example, the ability to predict weather conditions based on certain meteorological phenomena would be an example of application.

Level four, *analysis,* involves the breaking down of an idea into its component elements. In this manner communication of certain ideas can be enhanced and more readily understood. Also, the organizational patterns can be more clearly identified.

Level five is referred to as the *synthesis level.* This involves the putting together of parts to form wholes. Thus, pieces and parts may be so used and combined to form new patterns.

Level six is the *evaluation level.* This involves judgment and usually makes use of the first five levels. The use of some sort of appraisal standards is involved in order to make accurate qualitative and quantitative judgments about criteria.

---

*Benjamin Bloom, et al., *Taxonomy of Behavioral Objectives, Handbook 1* (New York: David McKay Company, 1967), pp. 7-8.

Turning to the affective domain, we find the emphasis on a feeling tone, an emotion, or a degree of acceptance or rejection. The categories of classification are divided into five parts.

Level one is that of *receiving*. The learner has to be sensitized to become aware of or attend to certain phenomena and stimuli. The effect of previous learning in the cognitive area is fairly easy to recognize, but the effect of learning on values and emotions is less obvious.

Level two, *responding,* is a more active type of affective behavior. It is characterized by compliance which may be a willing response to inner compulsion, possibly accompanied by some degree of emotional satisfaction.

Level three, *valuing,* is an abstract, internalized concept of worth. The learner has accepted a certain value after having been given several alternatives. He displays a certain behavior consistently. Eventually it becomes of value to him.

Level four involves *organization* of values. The learner arrives at a stage of internalization at which values are conceptualized. Then, a set of interrelated values may be organized to form a value complex.

Level five is *characterization* by a value or value complex. This is the highest level of internalization. The values already have a place in the learner's value hierarchy, are organized into some kind of internally consistent system, and have controlled the behavior of the learner for a time. Only when the learner is threatened or challenged does an evocation of the behavior arouse emotion.

In presenting a clearer picture of the taxonomy and the usable kinds of infinitives and objectives, Metfessel, Michael, and Kirsner have developed a table of behavioral objectives based on the framework of Blooms' Taxonomy.* The first column contains the taxonomic classification as developed by Bloom. In the second column appropriate infinitives are included. These may be consulted to assist in achieving more accurate and descriptive statements of measurable behavior. In column three direct objects relative to subject-matter manifestations are listed. It is hoped that this paradigm will serve to clarify and facilitate the development of appropriate behavioral objectives.

---

*Newton S. Metfessel, W.B. Michael and D.A. Kirsner, "Instrumentation of Bloom's and Krathwohl's Taxonomies for the Writing of Behavioral Objectives," *Psychology in the Schools,* Vol. VI No. 3 (July, 1969), pp. 227-231.

TABLE 2
Instrumentation of the Taxonomy of
Educational Objectives:
Cognitive Domain*

	KEY WORDS	
Taxonomy Classification	Examples of Infinitives	Examples of Direct Objects
1.00 Knowledge		
1.10 Knowledge of Specifics		
1.11 Knowledge of Terminology	to define, to distinguish, to acquire, to identify, to recall, to recognize	vocabulary, terms, terminology, meaning(s), definitions, referents, elements
1.12 Knowledge of Specific Facts	to recall, to recognize, to acquire, to identify	facts, factual information, (sources), (names), (dates), (events), (persons), (places), (time periods), properties, examples, phenomena
1.20 Knowledge of Ways and Means of Dealing with Specifics		
1.21 Knowledge of Conventions	to recall, to identify, to recognize, to acquire	form(s), conventions, uses, usage, rules, ways, devices, symbols, representations, style(s), format(s)
1.22 Knowledge of Trends, Sequences	to recall, to recognize, to acquire, to identify	action(s), processes, movement(s), continuity, development(s), trend(s), sequence(s), causes, relationship(s), forces, influences
1.23 Knowledge of Classifications and Categories	to recall, to recognize, to acquire, to identify	area(s), type(s), feature(s), class(es), set(s), divisions(s), arrangement(s), classification(s), category/ categories
1.24 Knowledge of Criteria	to recall, to recognize, to acquire, to identify	criteria, basics, elements

*Reproduced by permission.

TABLE 2 (continued)

| Taxonomy Classification | KEY WORDS | |
	Examples of Infinitives	Examples of Direct Objects
1.25 Knowledge of Methodology	to recall, to recognize, to acquire, to identify	methods, techniques, approaches, uses, procedures, treatments
1.30 Knowledge of the Universals and Abstractions in a Field		
1.31 Knowledge of Principles, Generalizations	to recall, to recognize, to acquire, to identify	principle(s), generalization(s), proposition(s), fundamentals, laws, principal elements, implication(s)
1.32 Knowledge of Theories and Structures	to recall, to recognize, to aquire, to identify	theories, bases, interrelations, structure(s), organization(s), formulation(s)
2.00 Comprehension		
2.10 Translation	to translate, to transform, to give in own words, to illustrate, to prepare, to read, to represent, to change, to rephrase, to restate	meaning(s), sample(s), definitions, abstractions, representations, words, phrases
2.20 Interpretation	to interpret, to reorder, to rearrange, to differentiate, to distinguish, to make, to draw, to explain, to demonstrate	relevancies, relationships, essentials, aspects, new view(s), qualifications, conclusions, methods, theories, abstractions
2.30 Extrapolation	to estimate, to infer, to conclude, to predict, to differentiate, to determine, to extend, to interpolate, to extrapolate, to fill in, to draw	consequences, implications, conclusions, factors, ramifications, meanings, corollaries, effects, probabilities
3.00 Application	to apply, to generalize, to relate, to choose, to develop, to organize, to use, to employ, to transfer, to restructure, to classify	principles, laws, conclusions, effects, methods, theories, abstractions, situations, generalizations, processes, phenomena, procedures

TABLE 2 (continued)

| Taxonomy Classification | KEY WORDS | |
	Examples of Infinitives	Examples of Direct Objects
4.00 Analysis		
4.10 Analysis of Elements	to distinguish, to detect, to identify, to classify, to discriminate, to recognize, to categorize, to deduce	elements, hypothesis/ hypotheses, conclusions, assumptions, statements (of fact), statements (of intent), arguments, particulars
4.20 Analysis of Relationships	to analyze, to contrast, to compare, to distinguish, to deduce	relationships, inter-relations, relevance, relevancies, themes, evidence, fallacies, arguments, cause-effect(s), consistency/consistencies, parts, ideas, assumptions
4.30 Analysis of Organizational Principles	to analyze, to distinguish, to detect, to deduce	form(s), pattern(s), purpose(s), point(s) of view(s), techniques, bias(es), structure(s), theme(s), arrangement(s), organization(s)
5.00 Synthesis		
5.10 Production of a Unique Communication	to write, to tell, to relate, to produce, to constitute, to transmit, to originate, to modify, to document	structure(s), pattern(s), product(s), performance(s), design(s), work(s), communications, effort(s), specifics, composition(s)
5.20 Production of a Plan, or Proposed Set of Operations	to propose, to plan, to produce, to design, to modify, to specify	plan(s), objectives, specification(s), schematic(s), operations, way(s), solution(s), means
5.30 Derivation of a Set of Abstract Relations	to produce, to derive, to develop, to combine, to organize, to synthesize, to classify, to deduce, to develop, to formulate, to modify	phenomena, taxonomies, concept(s), scheme(s), theories, relationships, abstractions, generalizations, hypothesis/hypotheses, perceptions, ways, discoveries

TABLE 2 (continued)

| | KEY WORDS | |
Taxonomy Classification	Examples of Infinitives	Examples of Direct Objects
6.00 Evaluation		
6.10 Judgments in Terms of Internal Evidence	to judge, to argue, to validate, to assess, to decide	accuracy/accuracies, consistency/consistencies, fallacies, reliability, flaws, errors, precision, exactness
6.20 Judgments in Terms of External Criteria	to judge, to argue, to consider, to compare, to contrast, to standardize, to appraise	ends, means, efficiency, economy/economies, utility, alternatives, courses of action, standards, theories, generalizations

TABLE 3
Instrumentation of the Taxonomy of
Educational Objectives:
Affective Domain

| Taxonomy Classification | KEY WORDS | |
	Examples of Infinitives	Examples of Direct Objects
1.0 Receiving		
1.1 Awareness	to differentiate, to separate, to set apart, to share	sights, sounds, events, designs, arrangements
1.2 Willingness to Receive	to accumulate, to select, to combine, to accept	models, examples, shapes, sizes, meters, cadences
1.3 Controlled or Selected Attention	to select, to posturally respond to, to listen (for), to control	alternatives, answers, rhythms, nuances
2.0 Responding		
2.1 Acquiescence in Responding	to comply (with), to follow, to commend, to approve	directions, instructions, laws, policies, demonstrations
2.2 Willingness to Respond	to volunteer, to discuss, to practice, to play	instruments, games, dramatic works, charades, burlesques
2.3 Satisfaction in Response	to applaud, to acclaim, to spend leisure time in, to augment	speeches, plays, presentations, writings
3.0 Valuing		
3.1 Acceptance of a Value	to increase measured proficiency in, to increase numbers of, to relinquish, to specify	group membership(s), artistic production(s), musical productions, personal friendships
3.2 Preference for a Value	to assist, to subsidize, to help, to support	artists, projects, viewpoints, arguments
3.3 Commitment	to deny, to protest, to debate, to argue	deceptions, irrelevancies, abdications, irrationalities
4.0 Organization		

TABLE 3 (continued)

Taxonomy Classification		Examples of Infinitives	Examples of Direct Objects
4.1	Conceptualization of a Value	to discuss, to theorize (on), to abstract, to compare	parameters, codes, standards, goals
4.2	Organization of a Value System	to balance, to organize, to define, to formulate	systems, approaches, criteria, limits
5.0	Characterization by Value or Value Complex		
5.1	Generalized Set	to revise, to change, to complete, to require	plans, behavior, methods, effort(s)
5.2	Characterization	to be rated high by peers in, to be rated high by superiors in, to be rated high by subordinates in	humanitarianism, ethics, integrity, maturity
		and	
		to avoid, to manage, to resolve, to resist	extravagance(s), excesses, conflicts, exorbitancy/ exorbitancies

Summary

Perhaps too frequently many teachers take the easy way out and teach without giving much thought to what they are teaching and what they hope the students are learning. It is quite simple to state, "I know my students are learning fractions" or my students really know how to regroup because I taught them the modern way." How does the teacher know the students are learning fractions? How does the teacher know that the students can regroup? A teacher, when writing behavioral objectives, must give some thought to her teaching and the effects it has on the students. This is true since the teacher must write the objective so that it states exactly what the student will be doing to demonstrate that he has achieved it. This means the teacher will know what she wants to accomplish and the most appropriate procedures to use.

The taxonomic classification developed by Bloom and the paradigm created by Metfessel are valuable tools which will aid the classroom teacher in planning and presenting effective lessons.

The taxonomy, divided into the cognitive, affective, and psychomotor domains, aids teachers in determining the class of behavior that students are to exhibit. The taxonomy also provides the teacher with a device for planning teaching strategies which do not deal exclusively with the low levels of cognition.

Metfessel's paradigm further develops the notion of the taxonomic classification scheme, offering the planner a number of infinitives and direct objects. This enables the teacher to translate the taxonomy into observable behavior, thus enhancing the effectiveness of the planning process.

A see saw instructor is a teeter-totter tutor.

Notes

CONCEPTUAL LESSON PLANNING MODEL

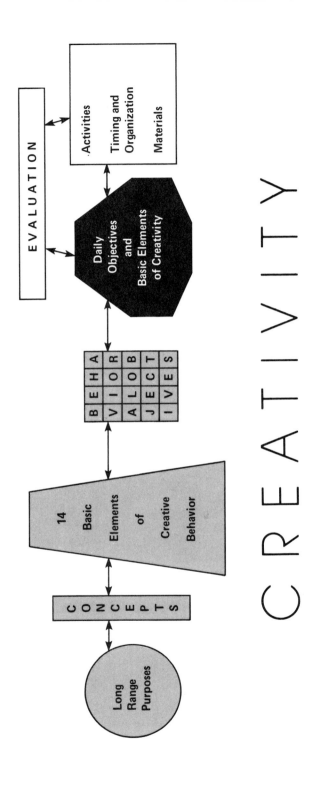

DAILY PLANNING

INTRODUCTION

So far, we have dealt with the important techniques of long-range planning. While critically important to the planning process, long-range plans are useless unless corresponding daily plans are developed for the purpose of implementing the master plan. Conversely, daily plans are virtually worthless if not utilized within a broader framework.

Let us reconsider the illustration of Coach McCool for a moment. You will recall that the main offensive weapon was an unstoppable all-American halfback named Seth Streaker. Let us further consider the two elements of Coach McCool's plans. First, he had a game plan which was to give the football to Seth and let him run. Second, since he was the fortunate possessor of such a magnificent running machine, he felt that his team's success depended on Seth's ball-toting talents. Therefore, each individual play was designed to set up openings so Seth could ramble. In other words, each play was called in terms of the total game plan. Passes were almost incidental. Their only purpose was to fool the defense.

You can see the analogy. In education, our "game plan" is the "long-range plan" while the "individual play" is the "daily plan." Daily lesson plans must be designed carefully to attain the long-range planning purposes. Take the incident in *Tom Sawyer,* when Tom found himself confronted with the perplexing problem of whitewashing a fence.

Immediately, Tom made a long-range plan. Just one. Very simply, he planned that someone else would whitewash that fence for him. The first incident (analogous to our daily plan) was Tom's imitation of a steamboat. This was convincing enough to trap Ben Rogers, then Billy Fisher, Johnny Miller, and so it went all afternoon. His creative, step-by-step (daily) planning helped him realize success in his long-range plan which was getting the fence whitewashed.

It might also be pointed out here that Tom Sawyer exhibited some mighty convincing motivational techniques! However, it is interesting to note that Huck Finn did not sally forth to help out on the fence. Perhaps he needed some kind of "super motivation" which even Tom Sawyer could not provide. This situation is not unlike many of our classrooms which contain a number of youngsters who are difficult to "turn on."

Part Two, then, will attempt to translate the long-range plans into functional, meaningful daily lessons. The five chapters discuss daily objectives, activities, organization, materials, and evaluation.

Notes

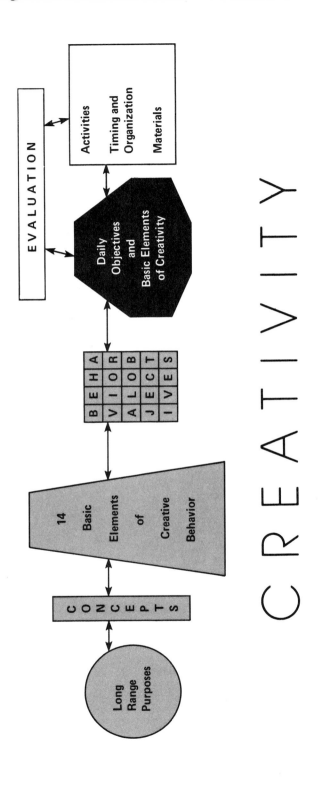

CONCEPTUAL LESSON PLANNING MODEL

EVALUATION

Activities

Timing and Organization

Materials

Daily Objectives and Basic Elements of Creativity

BEHAVIOR OBJECTIVES

14 Basic Elements of Creative Behavior

CONCEPTS

Long Range Purposes

CREATIVITY

CHAPTER FIVE

DAILY OBJECTIVES

Every undertaking must have some sort of objective even though in many instances the objective is either hazily defined or perhaps even unknown. When Sir Edmond Hillary decided to climb Mt. Everest, his objective was to be the first person to scale the summit of the world's highest mountain. While his feat had a very explicit objective, consider the process of rising in the morning. In this example, the objective is not even considered by the individual. It is practically an automatic reaction for most persons, and the objective is quite obscure.

Getting up is the thing to do. Nearly everyone does it, although often under protest! However, there are a number of objectives involved. For instance, one has to get up in order to eat, go to work, go to school, or merely to go out and play. A daily educational activity is a process similar to the examples cited above. In order to achieve a reasonable degree of success, it is wise to develop some sort of identifiable objectives.

At this juncture, it is important to point out the difference between behavioral objectives and daily objectives. You will recall our discussion of behavioral objectives in Chapter Two. Behavioral objectives pertain to things we want kids to be able *to do* in order to demonstrate that they understand the concepts we have been attempting to teach. Daily objectives are concerned with a plan of action which a teacher has prescribed for an individual lesson. The individual lesson is geared to the long-range plan. It is a prescription which should be carefully calculated to guide the learner so that he or she will be able to accomplish the behavioral objectives specified in the long-range plans.

Consider, if you will, a lesson which deals with a unit on the appreciation of American music. Two days are to be spent studying Ragtime. The objective for the days might be to familiarize the student with American Ragtime. In the daily plan, the focus is not necessarily on the behavioral objectives, although attainment of specific behavioral objectives might be measured on any given day.

In order to determine a particular daily objective, it is first necessary to consider long-range plans. A broad concept to be taught probably would be: "An important contribution made by Americans to the world's culture is its various styles and forms of music." One of the behavioral objectives derived from this concept might be: "The student can identify American Ragtime after listening to three records illustrating different piano styles." Therefore, this particular objective would coincide nicely with the long-range plans.

It should be remembered that the daily objective of a lesson should be flexible and readily adjustable. The daily objective can be derived through teacher planning, cooperative planning by students and teachers, or by the students alone. The objective of a lesson could develop from a question raised by the students in a previous lesson, or it could be some sort of task the youngsters have desired to tackle.

In developing daily lesson objectives the social climate of the group, the interests of the students, and their intellectual levels are all important subjects of consideration. As Bruner states, . . . "Any subject can be taught effectively in some intellectually honest form to any child at any stage of development."* Thus, the objectives must be realistic ones which lie within the level of the students' capabilities.

One element of ragtime, for instance, is that technically, rags combine musical form, melody, harmony, and most important, syncopation. To utilize this as a daily objective for a class of fourth graders, unsophisticated in music background, would be unrealistic. Unless the students possessed a thorough understanding of these terms, it would constitute an impossible daily objective.

In addition, it should be mentioned that a daily objective need not be confined to specific subject matter. Another type of lesson objective is concerned with the development of favorable attitudes or behaviors such as creative thinking, problem solving, cooperative work, imagination, or curiosity.

In order to assist students develop the creative thinking skills so necessary to the total educational process, we identified the Fourteen Elements of Creative Behavior which were discussed in Chapter Three. The principles to be developed should be identified with the

---

*Jerome S. Bruner, *The Process of Education*, (Cambridge, Massachusetts: The Harvard University Press, 1963), p. 33.

daily objectives in the planning process. One of the elements is fluency. By this, we mean that it is important to help the student develop some degree of familiarity with stored ideas which can be put to use in new situations. If a teacher wished to help children improve their creative thinking abilities, one objective for a daily lesson might be to help develop the child's verbal fluency.

Thus, it can be seen that the objectives which do not deal with a specific subject matter are of crucial importance and must not be overlooked in the planning process.

Summary

Every activity in which people participate has a purpose or objective. Some are quite apparent and discernible at the conscious level, while others are more subtle and are found at the pre-conscious or sub-conscious levels. Often these are never known to the individual. It is important that objectives be clearly thought out in each daily lesson.

Daily objectives are not to be confused with behavioral objectives. The daily objective pertains to a prescribed plan of action for an individual lesson. A behavioral objective is something we desire the learner to do in order to demonstrate that he understands a concept or generalization.

The daily objective should be flexible and easily adjustable. The teacher should encourage students to participate actively in the planning process. In developing the daily objectives, the interests and intellectual levels of the students must be considered.

Objectives should not be confined to the academic realm. Equally important are the objectives which pertain to attitude development, problem-solving skills, creative thinking, social skills, cooperative learning, imagination, and curiosity. Elements of creativity to be developed should be included with the daily objectives.

CONCEPTUAL LESSON PLANNING MODEL

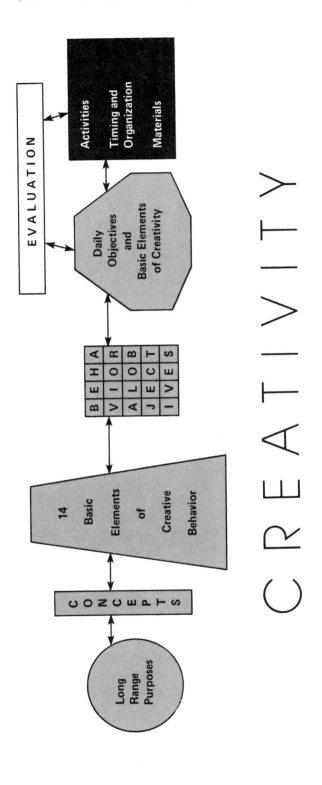

CHAPTER SIX

ACTIVITIES

Utilization of appropriate activities for the realization of particular goals is a subject of concern for many human beings. Babies go through a variety of activities prior to learning how to walk. They usually raise their heads, rock on their stomachs, sit up, crawl, stand by holding on, stand alone, and after a long series of tumbles, bumps, bruises, and considerable yelling and squalling, manage to take a first step. Each activity was carefully designed by nature, and each was suitable for the baby's development.

The surfer does not start out by attempting to "hang ten" on a twenty foot Hawaiian storm wave. First he learns to swim, he usually body surfs next, and finally learns to manipulate his board on a gentle two or three foot wave. Each activity is relevant for his stage of development. The emphasis, however, is on the appropriateness of the activity. The effectiveness of the activity is dependent upon the readiness of the individual to perform that particular task. You learn to crawl before you walk!

Another consideration is the difference in individuals. It would do a one hundred pound twelve-year-old boy very little good to work out with the sixteen pound shot put. On the other hand, it is equally doubtful that an Olympic shot put champion would benefit substantially by practicing with the junior high school boy's six pounder.

To draw the analogy academically, it is of little positive value to have a sixth grade student with a second grade reading level and a 78 I.Q. try to plow through the sixth grade social studies text. This would certainly be an inappropriate activity for her. Some other kind of meaningful activity must be provided.

After the level of individual difficulty has been determined, it is necessary to take a look at the activity itself. It is extremely discouraging to encounter this kind of classroom approach: "All right children, today we are going to study verbs. I want all of you to take out your language arts books. . . . QUIETLY! Turn to page 68.

Read pages 68 to 70, and answer the questions on page 71." Let us examine this all too common approach.

First, the phrase, "All right, children, today we are going to study verbs," does not exactly inspire anyone towards ecstatic enthusiasm. Before learning can occur, the learner must be motivated in some manner. For many students the motivation is almost a built-in commodity. Many youngsters desire to please the teacher and further motivation is seldom necessary. However, for many other students, additional motivation is required in order to activate the learning processes. A more exciting method must be sought and used.

Consider a second approach. Mrs. Livemore had a plan for teaching parts of speech to her fifth grade students who had watched their school team win the elementary league championship in football yesterday. This activity gave her an idea for a different approach to her lesson.

"How many of you saw the big game yesterday?" Mrs. Livemore asked. Everyone was there.

"What an exciting game that one was," said Frank. "I was afraid we wouldn't win it until Arnie Bowers ran that kick back for a touchdown."

"I felt the same way too," answered Mrs. Livemore. "I thought our boys did a fine job."

The class excitedly volunteered many comments pertaining to the big game. Mrs. Livemore continued, "I know that all of us were quite happy and excited about the outcome of the game. Let's see if we can think of some words that describe this victory for our school."

Many hands shot up around the room. Joe said, "It was a satisfying victory."

"A lucky victory," offered Nancy.

"An artful victory," John responded.

"The victory was a real smash," said the new girl from England.

"Wonderful," shouted Mrs. Livemore. Those are all excellent words. Those of you who haven't heard 'smash' used in that manner should know that this is a kind of English slang word which means that something is really . . . well, let's say . . . groovy. Now, could someone give me some sentences in which we could use 'smash' in other ways?"

Soon, a number of sentences appeared on the board:

1. The new star was a smash hit.
2. John tried to smash his brother's finger with the stick.
3. The bottle broke with a smash.

4. She returned the high lob shot with a beautiful forehand smash.
5. A fireman had to smash the window to enter the smoke-filled building.

"Let's see how this word can be used as different parts of speech," suggested Mrs. Livemore. The students noted that in sentence one it was used as an adjective describing the noun "hit." In sentence two and five, it was used as a verb, and the class reviewed the function of such action words in sentence construction. In sentences three and four, it was a noun.

So, in this particular lesson an entire concept was developed through the activity. The concept that Mrs. Livemore sought to develop was that one word can assume different language functions in varying situations. The activity she chose fit in well with her long-range plans for teaching parts of speech. Instead of a stultifying lesson in which the kids read and answered questions, Mrs. Livemore guided a lively learning activity which incorporated a number of key ingredients.

First, there was a playful quality to the lesson. Students were allowed to experiment with words. This instructional strategy is an important technique for developing creative thinking abilities. The enjoyable, relaxed climate encouraged the students to use their imagination.

Second, the teacher encouraged the use of divergent thinking abilities. She encouraged the students to explore different alternatives and examine them. While there are times when attention should be given to convergent thinking processes, this is too often the extent of classroom learning.

Third, the students were participating actively in the learning process. They were utilizing their own ideas and putting them into the classroom marketplaces for public observation and scrutiny. There was a willingness and an eagerness to become involved.

Fourth, the teacher established a non-authoritarian learning environment. There was an atmosphere of freedom to engage in unimpeded self-expression. Children were encouraged to explore within the limits of their own interests and abilities.

Finally, Mrs. Livemore encouraged creative thought processes. She promoted a classroom atmosphere in which the students were psychologically able to take intellectual risks.

At this juncture it is appropriate to interject a few comments on teaching styles, since they have a profound effect on classroom activities. It is possible to identfy three different styles. Style One stresses knowledge. The teacher who utilizes this method almost exclusively tends to cover the subject matter and the course of study. He is obsessed with "getting through the book" by the end of the year. The emphasis is on convergent thinking. Perhaps the prime purpose is to see that the students can memorize the facts and information. According to Bloom, "The most common objective of American education is the acquisition of knowledge."* Teacher One would tend to ask the question, "How long is the Amazon River?"

Style Two can be characterized by the question "Why"? Teacher Two would ask the question, "Why is the Amazon River important to South America and/or Brazil?" Teacher Two desires that students be able to use data to solve problems. He attempts to guide children into conceptual learning. Simply remembering that 9 x 9 = 81 is not enough. He wants his students to learn the number system, the laws of commutativity, inverse, etc. Knowing that the Polar Eskimos chew animal skins to make them more pliable is certainly an interesting fact, but hardly socially or historically significant. However, the concept that the Polar Eskimos probably migrated from Asia over an ancient land bridge is a crucial concept to consider. Teacher Two is more concerned with the latter notion.

Style Three goes still beyond and into levels of creative thinking. Teacher Three would ask the question, "What would happen to Brazil if the Amazon Basin got ten inches of rain for two straight years instead of the usual 200?" Her style of operation can perhaps be described as the "What would happen—if?" approach. Teacher Three is an independent thinker. She uses the ideas of others only as a stepping stone to the development of her own thoughts. She encourages this in her students. She is not too concerned with letter grades. Her classroom activities might deal with tasks such as playing "Twenty Questions." It is all right to fail in her class. *But* she sees failure as a positive learning experience. Just as the Federal Aviation Administration likes to find out why the latest airplane crash occurred, Teacher Three wants to know why Johnny can't find his prime numbers. Teacher Three will pick him up and help Johnny learn from his failure.

In planning these activities, it is important to see that they coincide with the long-range plans. In our earlier example, we considered a music unit dealing with the appreciation of American music. We wished to teach the following concept: "One important contribution made by Americans to the world's culture is its various

*Benjamin Bloom (Editor). *Taxonomy of Educational Objectives,* (New York: Longmans, Green & Co., Inc., 1956), p. 18.

styles and forms of music." Then we mentioned a possible behavioral objective: "The student can identify American ragtime as a form of music while listening to records." A daily activity might well consist of listening and discussion. The teacher would want to find some way of acquainting the student with different kinds of American music, pointing out ragtime music, and how it differs from other kinds. He would probably play a famous ragtime composition such as *Maple Leaf Rag* by Scott Joplin.

He would contrast this style with other forms of American music, encouraging the children to notice differences and similarities. After playing different rags, he would discuss the fact that rags were written for pianos, and eventually the children would become familiar with ragtime.

After having ample opportunity to participate in such activites, he would possibly play a number of records and see if most of the students could identify the ragtime records. Succeeding activities would deal with other kinds of American music. If the students could ultimately identify ragtime and other forms of American music, then the teacher has successfully guided the students toward the realization of these behavioral objectives. We can then assume that the students understand the concepts.

In examining criteria for determining the nature of various classroom learning activities, it is important to develop a rationale which can be useful for classroom teachers. At this point, let us consider a three part model which can be used.

Part one of the model is concerned primarily with the knowledge or data level. We will call it the information level. This is the starting point for the learning sequence. This kind of data input is necessary in order for the next two parts of the model to unfold. The learner merely stores factual information for later use.

Part two can be considered the processing level. One could draw an analogy of the data processing equipment which sorts information and puts it into some semblence of order. Part two is concerned with the translation and interpretation of the data acquired. The facts are sifted and analyzed in order to see what use is to be made of them.

Part three is referred to as the conceptual stage. The classroom teacher must attempt to assist youngsters in using the data with which they are familiar to formulate concepts. Some learning models also deal with the generalization and the principle. Quite commonly, the generalization is considered to be a number of concepts which form a more universal idea. The principle is considered to be a uni-

versal truth. As stated elsewhere in the book, we will concern our-
selves with just the conceptual level.

Even though the data level must be dealt with first, it is desirable
that in developing activities teachers move up the hierarchy from
level to level without dwelling too long at the data level. The following model should prove helpful:

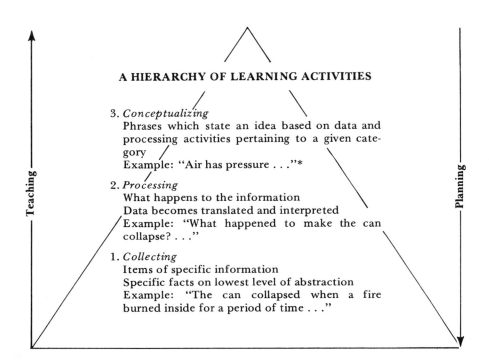

A HIERARCHY OF LEARNING ACTIVITIES

3. *Conceptualizing*
   Phrases which state an idea based on data and
   processing activities pertaining to a given category
   Example: "Air has pressure . . ."*

2. *Processing*
   What happens to the information
   Data becomes translated and interpreted
   Example: "What happened to make the can
   collapse? . . ."

1. *Collecting*
   Items of specific information
   Specific facts on lowest level of abstraction
   Example: "The can collapsed when a fire
   burned inside for a period of time . . ."

(left side: Teaching)   (right side: Planning)

It should be noted also that in planning activities, it is usually
wiser to begin with the concept. However, when implementing the
activity, the classroom teacher will normally start with the data and
work toward attainment of the concept.

In developing classroom learning activities there are a number of
principles to consider for determining what activities to choose. To
begin, it is necessary that the activity deals directly with the behavioral objective and concept being taught. For example, if the
concept being taught was: "Ideas are worthy of self-expression,"
then an appropriate behavioral objective for a first grade class using
the Language Experience approach in reading might be that, when

given a picture the student can relate his thoughts as the teacher writes them on a paper. An appropriate activity might be to have students verbalize their pictures to each other.

Activities must provide for multiple kinds of learning. When possible, the activity should provide for the mastery of more than one skill. For instance, if the topic is the Westward Movement, the class could be divided into three groups. Each of these could secure information about an ethnic group which came to the United States. Comparisons could be made about their differing life styles. In such an activity students would be gaining the following kinds of learning: (1) recall of knowledge; (2) the skill of comparing ideas and life styles through discussion; (3) development of attitudes; and (4) concept formation.

Activities should be developmental in nature when necessary. One activity should lay the groundwork for the next. It is imprudent to skip around without any specific goals in mind. This enables the student to proceed from the simple to the complex and from the concrete to the abstract.

Activities should provide for learning by many diverse means. Chapter seven will discuss some of the materials necessary for this kind of learning to occur. Basically, there are three general types of learning. First, some students learn best by reading printed matter. However, there are usually students in the traditional self-contained classroom who do not learn well this way because of reading deficiencies. These students might learn best by auditory methods. Still another group might perform best when confronted with a kinesthetic approach. At times, it might be most beneficial to use all three approaches. The choice is dependent upon the teacher's knowledge of the learning styles of his students.

Summary

In the consideration of appropriate class activities, it is necessary to consider differences in age, abilities, aptitudes, and the proper readiness level. In order to be meaningful, activities must be planned which are appropriate for individual class members.

Activities must have some sort of meaning for the learner. People need to be motivated before they learn. Little learning will occur during a dull, stultifying lesson.

A classroom environment should be established in which creative thinking can occur. A playful, easy-going atmosphere is probably most effective. The teacher must be careful not to become a dominant, authoritarian personality if a creative atmosphere is to flourish.

Activities should be designed which are appropriate for developing different levels of learning. Most question and answer sessions tap only the recall-recognition level of learning. Discussion activities should include more questions which ask "why" and "what would happen if?"

Daily activities must coincide with the long-range plans. The purpose of planning activities is to lead the learner to an understanding of the concepts which have been developed in the long-range plans.

Activities should be planned in terms of a three-part hierarchy of teaching. Level one deals with the acquisition of data. Level Two involves the processing of data. Level three is concerned with the ultimate development of conceptualization.

When determining appropriate classroom activities, four guidelines can be identified which should be of assistance to the teacher:

1. Activities should deal directly with the behavioral objective and concept being taught.
2. Activities should provide for multiple kinds of learning.
3. Activities should be developmental when necessary.
4. Activities should provide for learning by many diverse means, including the creative process.

A pair of brilliant surgeons
Sought some recreation
They got too high on pot and did
A joint operation

Notes

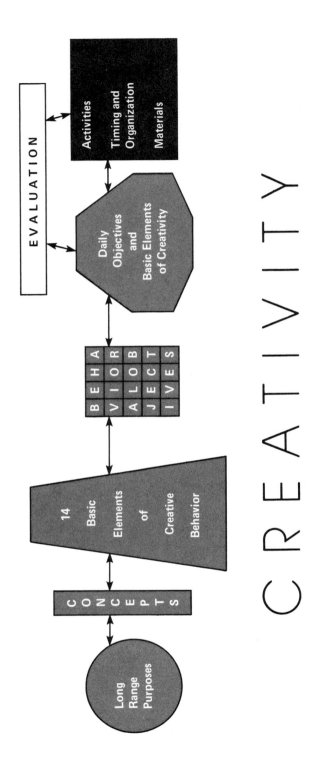

CONCEPTUAL LESSON PLANNING MODEL

EVALUATION

Activities

Timing and Organization

Materials

Daily Objectives and Basic Elements of Creativity

BEHAVIOR AL OBJECTIVES

14 Basic Elements of Creative Behavior

CONCEPTS

Long Range Purposes

CREATIVITY

CHAPTER SEVEN

TIMING AND ORGANIZATION

After considering the appropriate activity for the development of a particular behavioral objective, it is also necessary to plan for the proper kinds of classroom organization and timing for the procedures. Let's pursue this idea a little further by turning back to the story of Coach McCool.

Each spring, McCool would send out a letter to his potential football players, telling them when they should expect to report for their first practice. Each summer, he and his capable staff of assistants would map out their planning strategies and design appropriate activities. On opening day, McCool would line up his players and determine what kind of material was available. Hopefully, he would have a few glue-fingered young men about 6' 2" tall, weighing about 190 pounds who could go to 9.6 seconds in the hundred. These would be his flankers and split ends.

Usually, he would have four or five mean prospective tackles who were 6' 3" or taller, and at least 230 pounds in weight. Add a sprinkling of speedy six foot 230 pound interior linemen, a ten second 230 pound fullback, a Seth Streaker, a couple of quarterbacks who could think quickly and throw the football 60 or 70 yards with 60 per cent accuracy, and Coach McCool would commence to wring his hands in eager anticipation.

The coaches would first send all the candidates through a number of carefully designed fitness activities. They did a lot of calesthentics, took a number of laps, ran up and down the bleachers, and capped off the practice by running a mile in less than six minutes. The entire team participated in these activities. But then, the situation changed. The team was broken up into groups. Different linemen comprised one group, while additional groups were formed for the offensive backs and flankers, defensive linemen, and defensive backs.

Each group then commenced to work on various drills. The ends and flankers worked on pass patterns. Interior linemen tried to dislodge the tackling dummy from its moorings. The quarterback and the running backs worked on offensive timing—and so it went. We

Can draw a significant analogy from this description of McCool's practice sessions. First, he identified some activities which were appropriate for developing the various skills needed for different positions. McCool knew it would be silly for his defensive tackles to practice throwing passes, or to teach his quarterback how to block a punt.

Yet, when we enter the classroom of a teacher such as Mr. Green, we are too often greeted with the following example: "Okay children, today we are going to spend five minutes discussing some important things about George Washington. George Washington cut down his father's cherry tree, threw a dollar across the Potomac, and was the father of our country. Now, children, what were three things that George did?"

"He chopped down his father's cherry tree," volunteered Freddy.

"He threw a dollar across the P-Pa-Patomacka," offered Susie.

"Potomac," corrected Mr. Green. "Now, what was the other thing?"

"I know," Billy responded. "He freed the slaves."

"Wrong," shouted Mr. Green. "Now put on your thinking caps."

Andy's hand went up. "He was the father of our country," he answered.

"Excellent," beamed Mr. Green. "Now, I'd like you to open your social studies book and spend the next twenty minutes reading pages 31-40. Be sure to answer the questions on page 41. Remember, if you get all of them right, that's an "A!"

The students opened their books. Jeff Smart who had an I.Q. of 152, finished it all in ten minutes. George Plodder who had an I.Q. of 77 and a serious emotional block besides, was still trying to figure out what the letters c-o-n-s-t-i-t-u-t-i-o-n spelled on line two. Finally, he took the rubber band from his wrist, closed his book, stretched the band tightly, aimed it at Jeff, who was also in search of some meaningful activity, and let it fly. Jeff let out a yell and the merry-go-round had started again. Mr. Green shook his head after the day ended. "I wonder what went wrong today," he thought.

Perhaps Mr. Green could have spent some profitable time watching McCool's practices. The coach, unlike the teacher, realized that his players had a need for different types of activities. Therefore, it is crucial that in planning daily lessons, strategies be devised which will serve the very different needs of children. In order to accomplish this feat, close attention must be given to the type of classroom organization which is most appropriate, and also the proper amount of time to spend on various tasks.

The easiest and most common method of classroom organization is the one-group technique of working with the total class for the entire period. While this is appropriate and effective sometimes, it is commonly used in situations which could even cause serious psychological damage. Mr. Green's slow learner, George, could easily become defeated when he receives his "F" grade for not being intellectually able to perform a required task. If he consistently encounters learning situations in which he is destined to fail, the consequences could be disastrous.

A second negative consequence of the one-group approach can be illustrated by the reaction of another boy in Mr. Green's class. Ralph always had a tremendous interest in school. He had a vivid imagination, a keen sense of humor, a powerful curiosity, and outstanding intellectual ability. Indeed he was an exceptionally creative student. It is not difficult to imagine Ralph's reaction to this particular assignment of Mr. Green's. He greeted the task at hand with apathetic indifference.

From these two examples it can be seen that planning the timing and organization of the instructional sequence is crucial. Careful consideration must be given to the different ways of organization and how much time to spend in each phase. Some activities lend themselves to small group or committee work for short periods of time or for an extended time. In other instances it is appropriate to function individually, in pairs or trios, or occasionally in the entire group. The timing for these activities would depend on the objectives to be achieved. Perhaps twenty minutes is sufficient if an individual student is viewing a concept film on an eight millimeter projector or the entire class may spend fifty minutes watching a science film on atoms and molecules.

Several subject areas could be dealt with in all four organizational schemes. When presenting a unit of study on multiplication, the teacher might wish to begin with a general discussion with the entire group. The teacher might discuss the concept of multiplication being a short means of addition. Soon, some of the students would easily grasp this and other basic concepts. Perhaps this group would then be ready to study the distributive and associative laws as they apply to multiplication. Another group might need further work in the mastery of basic multiplication combinations. A third group might need to investigate the use of the zero in multiplication.

At some time, perhaps two members of a group might wish to undertake a specific project. For example, they might wish to study the method of multiplication used by the ancient Egyptians. Or, a

TABLE 4
Suggested Organizational Techniques
For Various Classroom Functions

	Individual	Pairs	Groups	Entire Class
Creative Problem Solving	x	x	x	
Reading Programs	x		x	
Mathematics	x	x	x	x
Social Studies Unit			x	
Music	x	x	x	x
Art	x	x	x	x
Language Arts			x	x
Science Research	x	x	x	
Science Problem Solving			x	x
Physical Education		x	x	x
Listening Skills		x	x	x
Speaking Skills		x	x	x
Spelling	x	x	x	x
Dramatics			x	x
Writing			x	x
Health			x	x
Development of Affective Learning	x	x	x	x

student might find it helpful to do some work with Napier's Bones. So all four forms of classroom organization could be utilized for maximum benefit. Again, the amount of time spent in the various organizational patterns would depend upon the objectives, the activities, and the progress of the students.

Perhaps the most important factor to consider in classroom planning is to insure that the *timing and organization of activities* is flexible. Students must be allowed to shift from group to group as the need arises. Sometimes a group member can work by himself for periods of time on special projects.

Finally, it should be mentioned that there is nothing sacred about all students working together in the same subject area for the same period of time. One of the most exciting elementary classrooms visited by one of the authors was a room of thirty youngsters of third, fourth, fifth and sixth graders. When entering the room, one was greeted with a wonderworld of fascinating projects. A listening center which could be raised to the ceiling by a pulley system was being used by six students: Two of them were listening to music, two were taking a spelling test, and two others were listening to a tape about space. About eight children were at their desks working on different subjects. Five others were painting a mural. The teacher wasn't in sight.

The door opened and two reporters from the class newspaper entered. They had just finished an interview with the principal. Suddenly, the teacher was spotted. He was kneeling in the corner with two boys who were making a crystal set. One student approached him and said, "Mr. Bright, I'm all finished."

"Okay, secret agent Q-T, get your orders from the box." The student went to the box and pulled out a sealed envelope. Soon he was busily engrossed in a creative writing exercise. The students were eager, and flew about their tasks with great gusto. In this instance, the program was individualized to the fullest degree and with great success. It was carefully planned, yet there was much flexibility in the timing and organization of the activities.

Summary

One important part of considering the kinds of classroom activities to use, is the organization of the class and the amount of time to be spent in various tasks. Sometimes it is more appropriate to work with the entire class, while other times it is more feasible to divide the class into groups or pairs, or to work individually. The timing and organization should be flexible and the teacher should be able and willing to change the organizational structure whenever appropriate. Children should not be "lockstopped" in one group. There must be provisions for appropriate movement between groups or the entire purpose of this type of organization is defeated.

Perhaps the biggest danger in classroom organization is in asking all the children to perform the same intellectual task which involves a large amount of reading. Since the average class will have a variance in reading levels of from six to ten years, individual differences cannot be met, in this manner and many children become easily bored or hopelessly frustrated.

CONCEPTUAL LESSON PLANNING MODEL

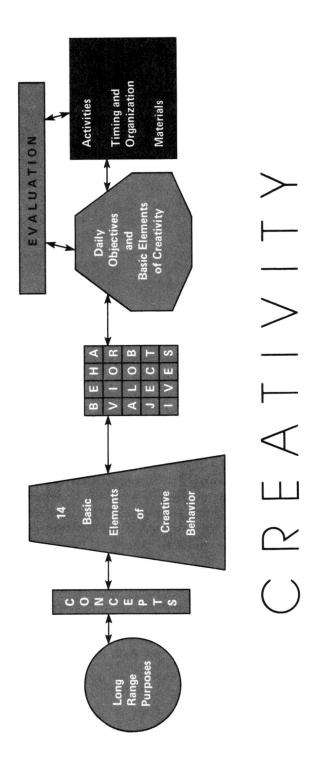

CHAPTER EIGHT

MATERIALS

Monday afternoon after a particularly bruising football game, McCool was threading the movie projector in preparation for the films he planned to show the team. It had been a grueling game last Saturday and his boys had played poorly enough to get upset by a mediocre team which they should have defeated by three touchdowns.

After showing the films of the previous game and those of Saturday's opponents, McCool turned to the diagram board. He went over individual mistakes, discussed missed signals, and finally finished his presentation by presenting strategies which would be utilized against next week's opponents. He gave the players a pencil and paper test on play signals.

Next, they moved outside. The linemen pushed the blocking sled and practically demolished the tackling dummy. They were a lot more fierce than they had been last Saturday. McCool directed the entire proceedings from his coaching tower, bellowing directions through his megaphone. The quarterbacks threw at the targets. His kickers took more than 100 practice place kicks from various angles and distances. The halfbacks practiced running around the tire barriers.

If you have kept track, Coach McCool used eleven different materials in this one coaching session. They were all ready for use when he needed them. He knew in advance what materials he would need for that particular practice session. He had developed a commendable degree of skill in using appropriate teaching methods and materials. Even though he lost that one game, McCool was an excellent coach. By using the proper materials and appropriate planning techniques, Coach McCool's forces rebounded brilliantly the following Saturday for a convincing win over a high-ranked rival.

Every teacher wishes to become an excellent one. But many fall short of their aspirations. This is true of the entire range, from the very finest who may also miss the goal occasionally, to the poorest who nearly always meet with failure and frustration.

There are varied reasons for this gap between a teacher's desired excellence and the actual performance level. In some cases the gap is caused by an inability to understand how students think. In others it is the result of limited knowledge of the subject matter or the inability to maintain order in class. But poor teaching is often due to a lack of skill in selecting and using teaching methods and materials.*

When teaching a social studies unit on the discoveries and explorations, the best experience a youngster could have would be to hop into a time machine and physically sail with Magellan or walk to the Far East with the Polos. Since this is impossible, the next best method is to provide some sort of vicarious experience which approximates the real one as nearly as possible. Obviously, lecturing and plowing through the textbook are probably the most ineffective means of approximating such an experience. While these two devices certainly are crucial in the total learning process, it becomes clear that other schemes must be utilized much more extensively then they are at present.

Colored sound films and television programs are extremely effective devices for assimulating the real event. Also effective are film-strips with a narrative record and prints which can depict a particular event.

However, there is an inherent danger in these particular audio-visual aids. If not used with care, they can become an end unto themselves rather than an appropriate teaching technique. The teacher who rolls in a projector, slaps on an unrelated film which he has never seen, rolls the film, wheels out the projector when finished, and continues without any follow-up discussion, is just as guilty of professional neglect as the surgeon who fails to scrub before an operation.

A film should serve to accomplish teaching objectives. Prior to showing it to students, the teacher should preview the film, take notes on the material, and make up leading questions for the students. The teacher should prepare the class for viewing by discussing the objectives with the students and presenting guide questions. The projector should be threaded and ready to go. After the showing, students should be allowed to react to the material and to establish verbally the main ideas presented. A discussion of the leading questions should occur along with an examination of conflicting points of view and a summarization of learnings.

---

*R. Murray Thomas and Sherwin G. Swartout, *Integrated Learning Materials* (New York: Longmans, Green and Company, Inc., 1960), p. 1.

Films and filmstrips can be used for a variety of purposes. They have great motivational value and can be used to launch a unit of study. Besides providing a source of information, they can constitute worthwhile supplemental materials and, of course, have great entertainment value. They can even be used in the summarization of a unit, as a problem-solving technique, and for evaluation and culmination purposes.

Other audio-visual techniques have an equally important effect on learning. Such devices as the overhead and opaque projectors, the bioscope, and tape recorder are valuable items. The use of puppets, records, tapes, exhibits, games, charts, and flannel boards help students develop values, character, and appreciation in a creative way.

When children become enthused about an educational task, some sort of physical involvement is usually necessary in order to sustain their interest. Therefore, it is important for the classroom teacher to provide saws, hammers, nails, wood, paint, and other such items. Sometimes this can be done as a class project with each student assuming the responsibility for providing certain things. Often, wood scraps can be procured free from the local lumber yard. It is imperative that plans allow for the provision of such items.

At this point it should be noted that children can listen to tapes of stories, music, plays, poetry, and even take spelling quizzes which are recorded. Other individual activities include the viewing of filmstrips and movies, listening to recordings, and the use of the opaque projector for the re-creation of maps and graphs.

In this segment of the daily plan, thy teacher must decide when it will become necessary to obtain the appropriate materials. Film ordering can be particularly difficult in school districts which have inadequate stocks. Such ordering must be done well in advance. In order for the lesson to proceed smoothly, such items must be available when needed. The teacher must plan for such materials in her daily planning sequence.

It is also crucial that the teacher continues to refer to the long-range plans and determine whether her activities are appropriate for leading to the attainment of the behavioral objective(s) tied to a particular concept. In like fashion, the materials used in the daily activity must be relevant to the particular task which the teacher has deemed important.

Occasionally, a teacher will plan for the use of many materials in a lesson without checking to see whether they follow the sequential flow shown in the planning model outlined in Chapter one. Sometimes principals or other people in a supervisory capacity will give the teacher the impression that it is necessary to bombard the students with a variety of materials in the presentation of a lesson. The teacher, anxious to stay in the good graces of such people for obvious economic reasons, tends to overpower the students with a multitude of media which may have little or no relevance to the task at hand.

On the contrary, it is necessary to supplement good lessons with the right materials, but in a realistic dosage. The patient who doubles the dosage prescribed by a physician does little to improve his health situation. Indeed, he can even hinder his recuperation by using such tactics. Similarly, the classroom teacher must write the correct prescription of materials for inclusion in her daily plans.

Summary

As a means of providing vicarious learning experiences for children, it is necessary to utilize a large number of audio-visual and other devices. Careful plans must be made for their use and adequate time must be allowed for previewing and preparation.

It is important that these devices be used as a learning supplement and not as an end in themselves. Films and other media have a variety of instructional purposes other than the conventional use of providing informational data.

The classroom teacher must continually consult the long range plans in order to make certain that materials are germane to the activities in accordance with the planning model.

Gross mistake: When you are supposed to ship 144 items but forget to include one of them.

Notes

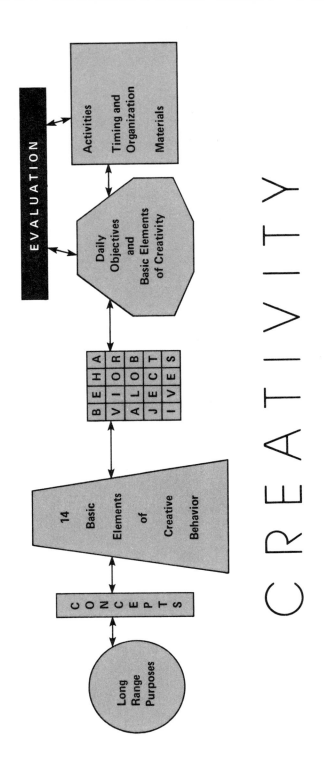

CONCEPTUAL LESSON PLANNING MODEL

CREATIVITY

CHAPTER NINE

EVALUATION

Coach McCool sat with his feet propped up on an empty trash can which he had turned upside down. He wondered if they would be ready for the championship game Saturday. With only one upset loss they had a chance to regain their number one ranking if they could squeeze out a victory. He replayed the day's practice. "I should have had them do more contact work," he thought. But then he considered the importance of having nobody injured for the big one. He needed everyone healthy.

"We definitely should have spent more time on that trap play," he muttered. "The timing still isn't quite right." He felt that everything else had gone quite well with one exception. The split end jumped three times on the new isolation pass play he had developed especially for this last game. He should have spent more time on that.

Then he reconsidered his goal for the year. He wanted to coach the number one team in the nation. And he still had a crack at it. Only the pollings taken after the big one would answer the number one question. And, it would take a good win Saturday to have a chance.

What our coaching friend was doing in his office was engaging in two types of evaluation. He was evaluating his daily practice and his ultimate goal for the season. He was trying now to decide how the practice went in general. And he was also wondering if the long-range goal of becoming number one could possibly be reached.

Let's go back to the classroom and consider the obvious analogy. The classroom teacher must do what McCool did. He must stop at the end of the day, put his feet up on the trash can, and evaluate his daily lessons. It must be determined whether he challenged the students and something must be done to shore up that boring lesson which put four students to sleep. He must try to determine why his discipline broke down. This is a daily self-evaluation and it must be done by the teacher each day. At this time, the teacher merely asks: "How did it go today?" This is the final section of the daily planning process.

But evaluation does not end with the asking of this question. In fact the question may launch an entire new area of study if the teacher feels that this would be appropriate. Daily evaluation is merely a means of providing feedback pertaining to the effectiveness of that day's lessons.

Another kind of evaluation must also be undertaken. In addition to the evaluation of the daily lesson, the long-range plans must also be evaluated. If the teacher did a good job moving from concepts to appropriate behavioral objectives, then long-range evaluation is quite simple. If most of the students could demonstrate the behavior changes as indicated through the behavioral objectives, then the unit of study was successful. If most of the objectives were not realized, then something serious went wrong. Perhaps the objectives were not stated properly. The activities could have been inappropriate for leading to those particular objectives. Not enough attention to proper timing and classroom organization might have been another reason. The task at hand could have been beyond the children's level of experience.

Therefore, when reading the remainder of this chapter, it is important to consider these two kinds of evaluation in much the same manner as Mr. McCool. He looked at the daily practice in terms of how it went generally, and he considered his long-range goals in terms of behavior. The classroom teacher must do this too.

Evaluation is often used to determine the strengths and weaknesses of students and the curriculum. It should also be used to give positive direction to the efforts of teachers. The effectiveness of the teacher will have much to do with the desirable changes that are made, or not made, by students. In this sense, evaluation should be used by teachers to make changes in their teaching. It should also help teachers to get better acquainted with their students in order to improve the learning experiences. If this is to be accomplished teachers must gather such evidence by using many evaluative devices.

One of the most common and useful is observation. This is also one of the most misused devices since it frequently consists of isolated incidents that the teacher especially liked or disliked and very little attention is sometimes given to the causes of the behavior. Teachers should realize that behavior is caused and they should search for these causes rather than attribute the behavior to the outward actions of the students.

A written anecdotal record can be used with observation. The anecdotes should be written accounts of significant student behavior in which the teacher writes exactly what was observed. When writing the anecdote the teacher should refrain from including his ideas of what caused the behavior in the specific situation. After several anecdotes have been written a behavior pattern will usually begin to emerge. This behavior pattern should begin to give the teacher some clues as to the actual causes of the student's behavior.

The following are examples of an anecdotal record written by a teacher who noticed that a student's interest in mathematics had begun to wane. During the first two months of school the student had been very attentive and was doing "A" work.

11/4

Angelita spent most of her time in math class drawing pictures or looking out the window. When she started to work on her assignment she finished it in ten minutes.

11/5

Angelita had five correct answers on today's work of twenty problems. When I asked her if she needed help, she didn't answer. I asked her to redo three of the problems while I watched. She solved all the problems correctly. During my explanation of the work for tomorrow, she was drawing pictures. She completed her work in ten minutes.

11/6

Angelita's work was better today—she had ten problems correct and twelve incorrect. While I observed, she answered correctly six problems she had wrong on her paper. She stated that she knew how to do the work but had been careless. It took her fifteen minutes to complete the assignment for tomorrow.

11/7

Out of twenty-five problems, Angelita had four right. She looked around the room and drew designs on her paper while the assignment was being corrected. I asked her to rework six of her incorrect problems. She did the first two correctly and then read a library book. She did not finish the remainder of the problems and did not take them home with her.

11/8

On the twenty-problem test given today, Angelita had a score of 90. She was the first one to complete the test.

These five anecdotal accounts indicate a behavior problem. Angelita was restless and inattentive during mathematics class. However, she seems capable of doing the assigned work. It is now possible for the teacher to begin looking for causes of Angelita's behavior.

The anecdotal record can also be used for group evaluation. In this setting the individual can further be evaluated in addition to the assessment of the total group behavior. The teacher again writes and collects non-judgmental accounts of individual and group behavior. A group behavior pattern should begin to appear after sufficient anecdotes have been gathered. These should provide valuable insight as to the causes of the problems within the group. The teacher can utilize this information to better understand the behavior of the group and what techniques should be used when working with it. In addition, it may give some added clues to the behavior of individual students.

Some of the causes of student behavior can often be traced to societal factors that are found both in and out of the school. Much research has shown that a student's academic development is directly related to numerous societal pressures that affect him. Family and school relationships, the student's self-image within the peer group, and the social atmosphere in our complex society, are all significant causal factors.

Since these and other social forces play such a tremendous part in a student's behavior, teachers should attempt to gather data concerning them.

There are numerous sociometric techniques that can be used to evaluate social relationships. Generally, these tools use some form of questioning and/or diagraming on an individual or group basis. The following are examples of sociometric devices that may be utilized to secure information concerned with parental and family relationships. (1) Compositions—any aspect of the home environment may be used as the focal point. Titles such as "My Family," "The Household Routine," "My Life at Home," "Father's (Mother's) Attitude toward School," can all be helpful in gathering information about home and family conditions. (2) Sentence completion—this tool provides another means of obtaining data about some of the influences found in the home. The following sentence stems illustrate this technique. When I talk about school my mother (father, brother, sister, etc.)_____. My family, compared with others, is_____. Mothers should learn that_____. I wish my father_____. My family treats me like_____. If I were a mother I_____. (3) Multiple-choice sentence stem is given with a list of alternatives. Examples of this type are:

Life at home (check one)   If only parents (check one)

_____is great   _____would make us study more

_____is sometimes great   _____would make us study less

_____is okay

_____ isn't great at all

Studying at home is (check one)   If only parents (check one)

_____very helpful   _____would make us behave

_____quite helpful   _____would trust us more

_____a waste of time   _____would pay more attention
                                        to us

When I talk about school my father (check one)

_____pays attention sometimes

_____usually pays close attention

_____always pays close attention

   After the data have been collected it can be tabulated by various methods. The type of tabulation would depend upon the sociometric instrument used and the problem the teacher is attempting to solve. (See Figure 8-1 on page 66.)

   Two areas of a student's school relationships are his feelings concerning teachers and his peer group. In order to obtain information regarding these topics a teacher could use any of the sociometric devices described earlier. Of course, there would have to be some modifications made. For example, in the composition technique, a suitable title could be "The Kids in this Class." My teacher thinks I

am_____could be a stem when the sentence completion instrument was given to students. Two examples of possible multiple-choice sentences are:

This class (check one)

_____is my idea of a great class

_____is okay

_____isn't very good

_____is terrible

When a teacher talks to me he seems (check one)

_____very pleased

_____somewhat pleased

_____satisfied

_____a little dissatisfied

_____very dissatisfied

Another method of gathering data dealing with social relationships in the classroom is to have individuals list the students they would most like to work with and the students they would least like to work with. The results of this sociometric tool can be tabulated on a matrix. (See Figure 8-1).

Figure 8-1.

student listed by assigned numbers

	1	2	3	4	5	6	7	8		26	27	28	29
1	−			+		+	−				+	−	
2			+	+		+				−			−
3		−		+			−	+		−	+		−
4	+				+		−	+		−	−		
5			−	+			+					−	−
6		−		+	+		−	+					
7		−					−	+			+	−	
8	+		−		+						−	−	
26	−		−		+	+		+				−	−
27	−						−	+				+	
28		+	−			−	−			+	−		
29	+			+	+	−		−			+	−	
total +	3	1	1	6	5	3	1	6		1	4	1	0
total −	2	4	4	0	0	2	7	1		4	3	5	4

The students are listed by assigned numbers on the top horizontal row and the vertical column to the left. Each row contains the choices made by the student whose number appears in the left column. For example, student number three chose students whose numbers are four, eight, and twenty-seven as individuals he would like to work with the most. Students whose numbers are two, seven, twenty-six, and twenty-nine have minus signs which indicate that student number three feels he would least like to work with them. A teacher, by adding the total number of plus and minus signs in each column, can readily see the choice pattern within a classroom. With this information a teacher can begin to ascertain the students who may need special help in improving their interpersonal relationships. A teacher may also use the compiled data, along with other information, in organizing students for group work, in discovering whether or not well-liked individuals are influential students, in finding out if well-liked pupils are cooperative with the teacher, in perceiving how the least-liked students feel about homework, etc.

Since successful human relationships facilitate the students' academic achievement and personal adjustment, it should be the teacher's responsibility to do everything possible to enhance the societal factors that operate in the classroom and school environment.

The teacher should be aware that one or two sociograms, used alone, are not valid in determining causes of behavior, likes or dislikes, feelings, etc. Sociometric devices should be utilized in a variety of situations that consist of both social and academic areas. Also, since the attitudes of students frequently change, the data may not be usable over a long period of time. The teacher, from his or her own observations, may therefore find it necessary and desirable to make adjustments as the need arises.

The following items should also be evaluated by the teacher: (1) The physical health of students. This should consist mainly of promoting a positive attitude toward healthful living and the detection of physical disorders that hamper learning. (2) The interests of students. Teachers should help students develop more and better interests. These new interests, along with those the student already has, should be used to foster learning. (3) The students' growth in effective work-study skills. The use of these skills, in conjunction with basic knowledge, is vital to learning. (4) The growth of critical and creative thinking. Most teachers realize that learning, to be useful, and valuable, has to be used in solving everyday problems. (5) The growth of self-concept. Self-concept can be a monumental motivational force in the students' learning and should be utilized as much as possible.

A word of caution is appropriate at this time. Teachers who use techniques that are designed to elicit "personal type" information should be aware that many school districts have policies restricting this type of questioning and testing. Teachers would be wise to secure approval of the proper administrator before attempting to gather such data.

Evaluative instruments that give results in quantitative terms are commonly used in academic and content areas. One of the most frequently used tests is an achievement test that measures the student's ability in such subject areas, as mathematics, reading, spelling, language, etc., and is standardized in terms of a norm for a particular grade level. An important factor to remember about this norm is that it indicates what the standardized group did, not what it should have done nor what it shouldn't have done. The norm is usually in the form of a grade equivalent divided into ten monthly seqments. For example, Billy Averageton, who is in the fourth grade, had a grade equivalent score of 4.2 on a reading achievement test that was administered during the latter part of October. This would indicate that Bill's achievement in reading is on par with his grade level placement. In other words, his score of 4.2 represents the reading achievement expected for average fourth graders after two months of school. Another type of score frequently used with grade equivalent is a percentile scale. If Billy's teacher would convert his 4.2 score to a percentile scale it would be found in the 50th percentile range. This score, 50th percentile, means that 50 per cent of all students taking the test made a score lower than Billy's.

Another standardized test commonly employed is the intelligence test. The general misuse of the results of these tests has caused much criticism. In some instances, students who early in their schooling, are "labeled" due to the score obtained may bear the stigma throughout their educational years. The score is usually referred to as the intelligence quotient or IQ. The use of this term has caused a great deal of misunderstanding and controversy in the field of education. A student's IQ does not measure his capacity for learning but only his mental growth and intellectual functioning at the time of the test. Educators often disagree on the constancy of the IQ and many teachers are confused by variations in test scores. Recent research has indicated that environmental factors can play a large part in the IQ. If children have not taken part in experiences that provide a background for learning (lack of parental love, use of paper, pencils, crayons, pictures, books, etc.) they usually tend to achieve below normal levels of expectancy. In addition to these factors, the results of the test may be varied due to the environment of the room (hot, noisy, interruptions); method of administration; physical and mental health of the teacher and pupils; and scoring of the test.

An important item to consider with the use of the IQ score is the age factor. For example, Billy Averageton's IQ average from a series of intelligence tests is 103 and his chronological age is 9-5. (Nine years and five months.) Sammy Stumble's average IQ is also 103 but his chronological age is 8-9. (Eight years and nine months.) Therefore, the MA (mental age) of the two boys is quite different. Billy should be ready for most fourth grade work, but Sammy may experience some difficulty with this level of work.

Although standardized tests are valuable tools, teachers should be cognizant of their limitations. Perhaps one of the most serious limitations is when teachers use a single achievement and/or intelligence score as the criterion for evaluation. No standardized test is a perfect measuring instrument and the manuals which accompany the tests tend to substantiate this fact. More teachers need to realize they cannot generalize from a test score since used alone it is often not valid.

Comparisons of students may also be an unfortunate use of test results. As was stated earlier, there are numerous variables that can affect the final outcome of a test. Therefore, if test scores indicate that one student has a higher achievement or intelligence than another student, the teacher should not use the test results as a basis for contrasting students.

Another factor that teachers tend to forget is that standardized test are not part of the normal classroom routine and student motivation is usually quite high when taking the test. Thus, many students perform better than they do on ordinary classroom work. Teachers should realize that most students cannot work at this high test level in the continuous day-to-day situation.

If the bounds of standardized tests, mentioned above, are kept in mind, the results of these tests can be valuable aids in helping teachers assess the knowledge of students.

Teacher-constructed tests are another tool that can assist in the measurement process. These instruments may include paper and pencil, oral, performance, and others.

The chief advantage of these tests is that, if properly constructed, they can evaluate behavioral objectives very effectively. The common forms of questions include (1) true-false, (2) simple recall, (3) multiple choice, (4) matching, (5) essay, and (6) problem solving. Of course, there are modifications that can be made in each of these types of questions and each of the various forms have certain advantages and disadvantages that teachers should consider.

(Since it is beyond the scope of this chapter to give a comprehensive analysis to the topic of teacher-constructed tests, the authorities cited below will enable interested individuals to do more extensive reading on this subject.)*

There are many purposes for using teacher made and standardized tests. Gruhn and Douglass** list the following: (1) to evaluate the teaching of the teacher, (2) to provide diagnostic information about students, (3) to evaluate the progress of the class as a whole, (4) to help students in their self-realization, (5) to plan for additional learning experiences, and (6) to measure the effectiveness of work-study skills. Regardless of the purposes, evaluation should be an on-going process, within teaching, that attempts to obtain as much information about students as possible.

The foregoing pages were concerned with the teacher getting to know students better. Both objective and subjective methods are used in collecting the necessary varied information and it may seem very time consuming. This is perhaps true, but the crucial question remains: *How can a teacher modify her teaching to bring about desirable student changes if very little is known about the student?* In many instances, the data described on the previous pages is kept in some sort of permanent form. A cumulative record or folder is commonly used for this purpose.

The cumulative folder is, perhaps, the most important of all the records that are maintained by schools. As pupils progress through school the information in this folder should be kept up-to-date and in usable form. Much of the knowledge that a teacher needs to have may be found in the cumulative folder. Such items as (1) personal data (name, date and place of birth, address, telephone number, and schools previously attended); (2) home and community information (occupation of parent(s), marital status, language(s) spoken in the home, number and age of siblings, and socioeconomic items); (3) records of tests (achievement, intelligence, aptitudes, interests, and personality); (4) school history (school marks according to grades and subjects, special reports, etc.); (5) medical records (physical dis-

---

*John A. Green, *Teacher-made Tests* (New York: Harper & Row, Publishers, 1963); Robert L. Ebel, *Measuring Educational Achievement* (Englewood Cliffs: Prentice-Hall, Inc., 1965), pp. 57-200; Jim C. Nunnally, *Educational Measurement and Evaluation* (New York: McGraw-Hill Book Co., 1964) pp. 91-165; Norman E. Gronlund, *Measurement and Evaluation in Teaching* (New York: The Macmillan Co.)

**Wm. T. Gruhn and Carl R. Douglass, *The Modern Junior High School* (New York: The Ronald Press Co., 1956), p. 319.

abilities, disease census, vaccination records, and up-to-date health records dealing with height, weight, hearing, eyesight, etc.); and (6) miscellaneous (notes from councelors, participation in extra-class activities, and anecdotal records from teachers and other school personnel concerned with developmental factors, citizenship traits, significant accomplishments, special abilities and interests, and abnormal personality characteristics) are usually found in a cumulative folder. With this wealth of information readily available, teachers should remember that the only use of the material in the folder should be to contribute materially to pupil growth and teacher understanding—not to compare or condemn.

It should be clear that the cumulative folder may contain much of the data that a teacher needs in order to evaluate the intellectual, sociological, psychological, and physiological traits of students. It is equally important that the behavioral objectives are evaluated in a manner which enables the teacher to determine clearly whether the students understand the learning concepts.

Let us now attempt to cite specific examples of how daily and long-range evaluation can be done in the typical classroom. At the beginning of the chapter, we discussed Coach McCool and the classroom teacher. You will recall we mentioned that at the end of the day the classroom teacher must put his feet on the overturned trash can, (this, of course, should only be attempted after sitting in his chair) and evaluate his daily lesson. In order to accomplish this task with some degree of success, it is important that he has some basic points to consider. Following is a list of items which should prove to be effective guidelines: (1) flexibility and creativity; (2) teacher-pupil rapport and control; (3) instructional pace; (4) appropriateness of procedures; (5) preparation for lesson plans and materials; (6) supervision of work; (7) provision for individual differences; (8) use of A-V materials; (9) explanation and questions; (10) student evaluation; (11) efficiency of routine; (12) enthusiasm and optimism; (13) tactfulness and judgment; (14) knowledge of subject; (15) communication.

Obviously, it will not be possible to consider all of these points in every lesson or perhaps even for an entire day. But they are all crucial elements of daily planning and should be considered carefully. Let's use Appendix B to cite an example. On Wednesday of the first week the objective is to provide initial opportunities for students to begin working in committees. You will see that a number of activities have been planned for the various committees. When the day is over, the teacher must use the guideline and determine whether the planned activities were successful in terms of the points under consideration.

Long-range evaluation procedures, on the other hand, require another approach. Let us re-consider Appendix B. In Section II, Learning Concepts, you will see that the first concept for consideration reads as follows: "Colonists and explorers brought values, goals, and ideals to this country which are still prevalent." In order to test this understanding, three behavioral objectives were developed. The first one was stated as follows: "The student will be able to trace at least one present day goal, ideal, and value of at least two religious, racial, and ethnic groups in differing geographic locations according to their historical beginnings." (For example, the settlers' dealings with the American Indians.)

After the teacher feels that the learning activities (found in Part II of Appendix B) have been completed, he must devise a technique for determining whether his students have attained the appropriate behavioral objective. This can be done in several ways. It could be part of a paper and pencil test which might be devised to check just this one or perhaps other behavioral objectives. Another possibility would be to allow the students to answer this question in essay form. It could also be done verbally. Other possibilities would be to create a mural, write a poem, write an ending to an unfinished story, or draw a cartoon.

The crucial question then becomes, what happens if these behavioral objectives are not attained by a number of the students. This could mean one of several things. Perhaps the activities were not appropriate in terms of the stated behavioral objectives. The timing and organization of activities might have been faulty. Perhaps more time was needed. Maybe another type of classroom organization might have been more suitable. On the other hand, the concept and behavioral objectives might have been too difficult for certain students. At this point, however, the teacher must decide if it is feasible to spend more time on the activities or organize them differently.

In order to meet the individual needs of students it might be necessary to further reorganize the classroom. Students who have not yet attained the prescribed behavioral objectives might need to do some additional work. However, if the youngsters were able to succeed in mastering the behavioral objectives, the teacher is safe in assuming that the concepts are sufficiently understood and that the unit of study has been successful. The teacher and her students are ready to move on to new areas of study.

Summary

In terms of the planning sequence, evaluation must be considered in two different ways. First, the daily lessons must be evaluated by the teacher each day. This kind of evaluation is not usually made by checking on the attainment of behavioral objectives. Rather, it is a consideration of the general effectiveness of the activities and their timing and organization. The evaluation of the long-range purposes in the planning sequence comes either at the end of the unit or at intervals along the way. This kind of evaluation is relatively simple. It is done by checking the behavioral objectives and deciding whether the student has been able to perform the prescribed tasks. If he has, the teacher is safe in assuming that the student understands the concepts she has been trying to teach. If not, she needs to reexamine her daily activities, her timing and organization, and the difficulty level of the concepts.

Evaluation should consist of the accumulation of comprehensive evidence concerned with the behavioral changes that students demonstrate in mental, social, emotional, and physical development. To accomplish this the teacher must form the habit of using many data-gathering techniques. Evaluation truly becomes effective when many methods are used.

Very little progress can be made toward attempting to make desirable behavioral changes occur in students until pertinent information is obtained about them. The evaluation process should be taking place while the teacher is with the students, and not only when tests are given. Stated more briefly, evaluation is not something that is done only after teaching, but it should take place simultaneously with teaching, and even before teaching when preassessments are made of students.

SOCIAL STUDIES (Secondary)

PART 1

LONG-RANGE PLANS

I. LONG-RANGE PURPOSES

A. To acquaint the students with the factors which determine many of the cultural living patterns of people.
B. To broaden the student's understanding of his own environment.

II. LEARNING CONCEPTS

A. Early cultures were shaped to a great extent by their climatic surrounding.
B. Early cultures were greatly influenced by the geographic environment in which they existed.
C. Certain societal factors are universal to all cultures (religion, food, shelter, clothing, government, transportation, etc.).
D. Man's language provides him with the means of expressing the essence of his culture.

III. ELEMENTS OF CREATIVE BEHAVIOR

A. Originality (#4)
B. Development of Humor (#1)
C. Resourcefulness (#10)
D. Imagination (#13)

IV. BEHAVIORAL OBJECTIVES

(Learning Concept A)
A. The student will be able to compare civilizations found in the Kalahari Desert, the Amazon Basin, the Sierra Madres, and the Yangtze River Valleys, by identifying the similarities and differences of their climatic conditions as they effect their food, clothing, and shelter.

B. The student will be able to identify at least five characteristics of the four major areas which are caused by their climatic surroundings.

C. The student will be able to compare at least one societal norm from each of the four cultures which might exist to some degree because of its climate.

(Learning Concept B)

A. The student will be able to identify at least five characteristics of the four major areas which are caused by their geographic circumstances.

B. The student will be able to contrast the four major areas by identifying the similarities and differences in their geographic conditions as they effect food, clothing, shelter, and transportation.

C. The student will be able to compare at least one societal norm from each of the four cultures which might exist to some degree because of its geographic environment.

(Learning Concept C)

A. The student will be able to identify at least five societal factors which are common to all four cultures.

B. The student will be able to debate which culture has the most sensible mores.

(Learning Concept D)

A. The student will be able to identify at least three kinds of ideas which can be communicated through language.

B. The student will be able to theorize how ideas could be presented in an absence of verbal language by identifying at least five ways in which animals communicate.

C. The student will be able to analyze verbally his views on the function of language as a means of portraying man's cultural essence.

(All Learning Concepts)

A. Based on the learned information pertaining to the four societies, the student will be able to develop a culture based on certain prestated conditions relating to weather and climate. This culture will describe the people's religion, food, clothing, shelter, government, transportation, music, art, and sports.

V. EVALUATION

If the students are able to attain these instructional objectives, the teacher can safely assume that they understand the concepts. If not, the planning sequences must be retraced. Either the concepts are unattainable for students, and/or the daily activities were not appropriate for the objectives developed.

PART 2

DAILY PLANS

MONDAY—FIRST WEEK

Objective: To introduce the topic of study.

Elements of Creative Behavior:

1. Originality (#4)
2. Imagination (#14)

Activities: After briefly introducing the topic, the principles of brainstorming are introduced. A practice session is conducted with the large group. Then, groups of three will brainstorm possible answers to the following questions:

1. What do you think (name each of the four areas) is like in terms of their geographic characteristics.
2. What do you think (name each of the four areas) is like as a result of their climatic conditions.

Timing and Organization: The introduction will take ten minutes with the entire classroom together. Then, after a fifteen minute practice brainstorming session, the students will be divided into trios for small group brainstorming related to the preceding two questions for 30 minutes.

Materials: Chalkboard and chalk, papers and pencils.

Evaluation: Teacher determines whether opening session was appropriate.

TUESDAY-FRIDAY—FIRST WEEK

Objective: To familiarize the students with the general characteristics of the four cultures.

Elements of Creative Behavior:

1. Resourcefulness (#10)

Activities: Students will be divided into four research groups. Each group, through the use of encyclopedias, almanacs, flora and forms maps, atlases, and resource people, will gather data pertaining to their area of study. Research groups will explore in depth, the topic areas indicated in the behavioral objectives. Students will utilize the facilities of local libraries, and other local education institutions in order to gather the materials. Progress will be evaluated daily after the session.

Timing and Organization: Students will be in four groups. The introduction and evaluation portion will take ten minutes which will provide forty minutes for the activity itself.

Materials: Resource materials as identified by students and teacher. (Must include all topics stated in the behavioral objectives.)

Evaluation: Each committee will participate in an oral progress evaluation of their progress.

MONDAY-TUESDAY—SECOND WEEK

Objective: To provide students with an opportunity to create an artistic production depicting the culture on which they are reporting.

Elements of Creative Behavior:

1. Originality (#4)
2. Imagination (#14)

Activity: Each committee will choose a means of creating an artistic replication of their culture. This could be accomplished through the production of a mural, creation of a diorama, making a model relief map, etc. (See Monday-Tuesday, Third Week.)

Timing and Organization: Students will spend the first 5 minutes together in planning activities, 45 minutes working, and the final 5 minutes in evaluation.

Materials: Necessary art and construction materials.

Evaluation: Discuss progress on the various projects.

WEDNESDAY-THURSDAY—SECOND WEEK

Objective: To provide the students with an opportunity to create humorous works related to the culture they are studying.

Elements of Creative Behavior:

1. Humor (#1)
2. Originality (#4)
3. Imagination (#14)

Activities: Students will be given input on the pun and other forms of humor. The teacher might read the following pun-poem relating to another culture on the African continent:

"Long ago in Egypt
Lived an osteopathic actor
And he gained wealth and fame
As the hammy 'Cairo' practor!"
by David Mitchell

Other short humorous stories, puns, and pun-poems will be read
and discussed. Students will then work in small groups and create
their own humorous works for sharing at the end of the Thursday
period.

Timing and Organization: Students will be together for input sessions, then will work in groups of three.

Materials: Pencil and paper, overhead projector and screen for discussion of humorous works.

Evaluation: Will be based on the quality of the humorous works,
through a process of self-assessment.

FRIDAY—SECOND WEEK

Objective: To acquaint students with the manner in which language
serves as a device which captures the essence of a culture.

Elements of Creative Behavior:
1. None in particular.

Activities: Students will be given the opportunity to view a videotape depicting the cultural conditions of the Chicano Child. They
will see a tape and participate in a group discussion focusing on
the content.

Timing and Organization: The entire period, students will be working in one large group.

Materials: Videotape and VTR playback apparatus.

Evaluation: Based on student participation during group discussion.

MONDAY—THIRD WEEK

Objective: To assist students in preparing a class presentation.

Elements of Creative Behavior:
1. Resourcefulness (#10)
2. Originality (#4)
3. Imagination (#13)

Activities: Students will work in their cultural study group and pre-
pare a presentation for the entire class.
Timing and Organization: 5 minutes in giving direction, 45 in prepa-
ration (in four groups) and 5 in evaluation.
Materials: None.
Evaluation: Completion of presentation planning.

TUESDAY – THIRD WEEK

Objective: To present a summary of each culture studied to the
entire group.
Elements of Creative Behavior:
1. Resourcefulness (#10)
2. Originality (#4)
Activities: Each of the four groups will give a group presentation
based on their research findings and their artistic depiction of the
culture.
Timing and Organization: Each group presentation will take no
more than twelve minutes.
Materials: Props as needed by each group.
Evaluation: Effectiveness of the presentation.

WEDNESDAY – THIRD WEEK
THURSDAY – FOURTH WEEK

Objective: To have students use the data they now have in creating a
new culture when provided with certain geographical and climatic
conditions.
Elements of Creative Behavior:
1. Resourcefulness (#10)
2. Originality (#4)
3. Imagination (#14)
Activities: Each group will prepare a written report and a visual
reproduction of the culture they are creating. A presentation will
be given to the class describing their culture's religion, food, clothing, shelter, government, transportation, sports, art, music, and
language.
Timing and Organization: Each of the four groups will be given a
description of a climatic/geographical environment *different* from
the one already studied. They will work in their groups doing the

necessary research, art activities, and preparation of the report. A ten minute pre- and post-activity period will be utilized for giving directions and evaluating progress.

Materials: Research and art materials as needed.

Evaluation: Based on daily group progress.

FRIDAY—FOURTH WEEK

Objective: To present a summary of each culture studied to the entire group.

Elements of Creative Behavior:

1. Resourcefulness (#10)
2. Originality (#4)

Activities: Each of the four groups will give a group presentation based on their research findings and their artistic depiction of the culture.

Timing and Organization: Each group presentation will take no more than twelve minutes.

Materials: Props as needed by each group.

Evaluation: Effectiveness of the presentation. Teacher will also assess the attainment of the behavioral objectives identified in the long-range portion of the plans by periodic evaluation at appropriate times.

APPENDIX B

PHYSICAL EDUCATION—BODY MOVEMENTS (Elementary)

I. LONG-RANGE PURPOSES

    A. To develop an understanding of how the human body moves in different ranges.

    B. To develop an understanding of how the human body can change shapes.

II. LEARNING CONCEPTS

    A. The human body is an instrument of movement since it has shape at any given position.

    B. Movement is attained by a change in shape.

    C. Space, force, time, and flow are elements of movement.

    D. The dimensions of space are directions, planes, levels, and ranges.

    E. Four types of body shapes are straight and narrow, rounded, straight and wide, and twisted.

    F. Range is the relationship of the body to personal space.

III. ELEMENTS OF CREATIVE BEHAVIOR

    A. Self-Concept (#6)

    B. Resourcefulness (#10)

    C. Originality (#4)

IV. BEHAVIORAL OBJECTIVES

(Learning Concept A)

    1. The student will be able to make and hold five different body shapes.

(Learning Concept B)

    1. The student will demonstrate eight different shapes while maintaining flow in movement.

(Learning Concept C)

1. While doing a two minute routine of his own choosing, the student will demonstrate each of the four elements of movement.

(Learning Concept D)

1. The student will be able to move in three different levels and three directions.
2. The student will demonstrate three different ranges in space.
3. The student will demonstrate three different planes in space.

(Learning Concept E)

1. The student will demonstrate two straight and narrow body shapes.
2. The student will demonstrate two straight and wide body shapes.
3. The student will demonstrate two rounded body shapes.
4. The student will demonstrate two twisted body shapes.

(Learning Concept F)

1. The student will be able to identify the difference between large and small movements.
2. The student will be able to explain at least two different feelings when the body is fully extended.

V. EVALUATION

If students are able to attain the stated behavioral objectives, the teacher can assume that they have learned the concepts. If not, the planning sequence should be reviewed. Either the concepts were too difficult to achieve and/or the daily activities were not sufficient or appropriate for the objectives listed.

PART 2

DAILY PLANS

MONDAY—FIRST WEEK

Objective: To introduce the ideas of range and shape in movement.
Elements of Creative Behavior:
1. Self concept (#6)
Activities:
1. Introduce and demonstrate the ideas of range and shape.
2. Have students move in the general space of the area using the biggest movements possible.
3. Have pupils move with the smallest movements possible.
4. Individuals will demonstrate big and small movements and describe how these movements could be changed.

Timing and Organization: The introduction and demonstration will take five minutes. Allow ten minutes for the big and small movement experimentation. The last twenty minutes will be spent in individual demonstrations and explanations. (Teaching time is thirty-five minutes which does not include dressing, roll, warm-ups, showers, etc.)

Materials: A large room (gym) or outside space and appropriate clothing for students.

Evaluation: Assessment of individual's own movements and teacher observation.

TUESDAY—FIRST WEEK

Objective: Introduce the concept of personal space within a given general area.
Element of Creative Behavior
1. Self concept (#6)
Activities:
1. Instruct students to move in general space using large movements and come as close as possible to another person before springing away.
2. Add to this by having pupils do backward, sideways, levels, and direction changing movements.

3. Using a checklist and written evaluation, have individuals evaluate the dimensions of space, types of body shapes, and range they utilized. The written evaluation should include how these could have been improved.

Timing and Organization: Instructions and demonstrations by teacher will take five minutes. Student activities involving movements will be twenty minutes. The time for self-evaluation will be ten minutes.

Materials: Large open area and appropriate clothing for students.

Evaluation: Self-assessment utilizing checklist and written evaluation; also teacher observation and positive comments.

WEDNESDAY—FIRST WEEK

Objective: To develop the control of force, range, and flow of body movements in limited space. To introduce the use of balls while moving in different shapes and ranges.

Element of Creative Behavior:

1. Originality (#4)

Activities:

1. Teacher will demonstrate shapes and ranges of movement while controlling a ball.

2. Have students practice moving within their personal space while controlling a ball.

3. After practicing, have individuals think of as many movements as possible in which they can use to control a ball or balls in a limited shape.

4. Allow pupils who volunteer to demonstrate their ball control movements.

Timing and Organization: Demonstration by teacher will be five minutes in length. Student practice session and time for developing new movements will last twenty minutes. Demonstrations by individuals will be for ten minutes.

Materials: Large area, appropriate clothing for students, and sufficient balls of various sizes.

Evaluation: None.

THURSDAY – FIRST WEEK

Objective: To review previous learning concepts and introduce the idea of a partner in using movements.

Element of Creative Behavior:

1. Originality (#4)

Activities:

1. Teacher explanation and demonstration of previous learning concepts.
2. Have students pick partner and move about the general space with each other.
3. Have students develop a unique, one-minute routine that utilizes as many of the previous body movements as possible.
4. Pairs will demonstrate their routines to the class.

Timing and Organization: Five minutes for demonstrations and explanations by teacher. Student moving about with partner and development of routine will take fifteen minutes. Demonstrations of routines by pairs of students will be for fifteen minutes.

Materials: Large area and appropriate clothing for students.

Evaluation: Participation of students while working in pairs; teacher observation.

FIRDAY – FIRST WEEK

Objective: To review the various shapes (straight and narrow, straight and wide, rounded, twisted) that can be used in movement and to develop routines utilizing flow and at least two of each type of shape.

Element of Creative Behavior:

1. Originality (#4)

Activities:

1. Demonstration by teacher on each of the four shapes.
2. Have students explore doing as many variations of the shapes as they can.
3. Let volunteers demonstrate their variations and discuss other possibilities.
4. Students, working individually or in pairs, will develop original routines that utilize shapes and flow and will be from one to two minutes in length.

Timing and Organization: Teacher demonstration will last five minutes. Explorations of various shapes and demonstrations by volunteers will take fifteen to twenty minutes. Students will spend the remainder of the period in developing their routines.

Materials: Large area and appropriate clothing for students.

Evaluation: Degree of student participation.

MONDAY–SECOND WEEK

Objective: Have students demonstrate routines.

Element of Creative Behavior:

1. Originality (#4)

Activities:

1. Demonstrations by students, either in pairs or individually, of their routines.

Timing and Organization: Entire period will be spent on presentations by students (thirty-five minutes).

Materials: Large area and appropriate clothing for students.

Evaluation: Degree of student participation.

TUESDAY–SECOND WEEK

Objective: To provide students with further information on educational gymnastics.

Element of Creative Behavior:

1. None

Activities:

1. Show a film dealing with body movements. A discussion concerned with the elements of movement will take place after the film. (Students will be alerted to the idea that while viewing the film, and during the discussion, they should keep in mind ideas they could use in a creative body movement routine.)

Timing and Organization: The entire thirty-five minutes will be spent on the two activities.

Materials: Appropriate film on body movements (content, length, etc. of film would depend on students), and projector.

Evaluation: None.

WEDNESDAY, THURSDAY–SECOND WEEK

Objective: To have students develop a creative body movement routine that would emphasize a theme.

Elements of Creative Behavior:

1. Self-concept (#6)
2. Resourcefulness (#10)
3. Originality (#4)

Activities:

1. Teacher will explain guidelines for routines—may be done individually, in pairs, or small groups.
2. Students may utilize objects other than their bodies.
3. All movements stated in behavioral objectives should be included.
4. Routine should have a theme.

Timing and Organization: Ten minutes will be used for explanations by the teacher. During the remaining time, students will work on their routines.

Materials: Large area, appropriate clothing for students, and any objects requested by students.

Evaluation: None at this time.

FRIDAY–SECOND WEEK (to conclusion of routines)

Objective: Have students present routines.

Elements of Creative Behavior:

1. Self-concept (#6)
2. Resourcefulness (#10)
3. Originality (#4)

Activities:

1. Students will present their body movement routines.

Timing and Organization: This will depend on the routines given by students.

Materials: Large area, clothing for students, and any objects requested by students.

Evaluation: Each student will critique their own performance stressing strengths, weaknesses, and areas for improvement.

AIR (Elementary)

I. LONG-RANGE PURPOSES

A. To develop the understandings of characteristics and properties of air.
B. To develop basic understandings of the uses of air.
C. To enhance creative thought production through use of the scientific method.

II. LEARNING CONCEPTS

A. Air occupies space.
B. Air has weight.
C. Air exerts pressure in all directions.
D. Air expands when heated.
E. Air contracts when cooled.
F. Air pressure is useful to man.
G. The scientific method is a means of solving problems through the use of creativity.

III. ELEMENTS OF CREATIVE BEHAVIOR

A. Fluency (#2)
B. Elaboration (#5)
C. Experimenting with and Testing Ideas and Hunches (#7)
D. Learning from Failure (#8)
E. Resourcefulness (#10)
F. Problem Sensitivity (#11)

IV. BEHAVIORAL OBJECTIVES

(Learning Concept A) Through the use of the scientific method the student will be able to:
1. perform at least two experiments which demonstrate that air occupies space;

    2. explain verbally at least two experiments which show that air occupies the space that is not occupied by any other substance;

(Learning Concept B)

    1. interpret at least two experiments which prove that air has weight;

(Learning Concept C)

    1. perform at least two experiments which prove that air exerts pressure in all directions;

(Learning Concept D)

    1. analyze verbally at least two experiments which demonstrate that air expands when heated;

(Learning Concept E)

    1. explain at least two experiments which prove that air contracts when cooled;

(Learning Concept F)

    1. identify ten ways that air pressure is useful to man;

    2. deduce what life would be like if air had no pressure;

(Learning Concept G)

    1. perform successfully in attainment of the first six objectives which involve the use of creative, scientific problem-solving processes.

IV. EVALUATION

A. If the students are able to accomplish the above objectives, the teacher can assume that they understand the concepts.

PART 2

DAILY PLANS

MONDAY–FIRST WEEK

Objective: To introduce the study of air.

Elements of Creative Behavior:
1. Fluency (#2)
2. Problem Sensitivity (#11)

Activities: After an opening introduction, the film *Experimenting With Air* will be shown. Following a discussion of the film, students and teacher will plan future activities.

Timing and Organization: The introduction will take about five minutes with the entire class working in one group. The film takes about 13 minutes. The last ten or twelve minutes will be used to discuss the film and plan future activities.

Materials: Film: *Experimenting With Air* from International Film Bureau, 1 16mm sound projector, and 1 screen.

Evaluation: The teacher will determine through observation whether the procedure was a success and whether the planning was sufficient.

TUESDAY–FIRST WEEK

Objective: To determine the procedure for experimentation and demonstration of the learning concepts.

Elements of Creative Behavior:
1. Resourcefulness (#10)

Activities: The children will help list questions and brainstorm possible solutions. Yesterday's film should motivate and inspire the students. The teacher will interject essential questions which are related to the learning concepts.

Timing and Organization: The class will work together for the entire 30 minutes on this activity.

Materials: No special materials are needed for this lesson.

Evaluation: The teacher will decide after careful inventory whether all pertinent questions have been included.

WEDNESDAY—FIRST WEEK

Objective: To lead the students to discover and understand that air
occupies space.

Elements of Creative Behavior:

1. Experimenting with and Testing Ideas and Hunches (#7)
2. Learning from Failure (#8)
3. Resourcefulness (#10)

Activities: The teacher will involve students in the following demonstrations while leading a discussion as to WHAT is happening,
WHY, and WHAT DOES THIS TELL US about air:

1. Blow up a balloon. Hypothesize, observe, and discuss.
2. Place a glass tumbler upside down into a pan of water. Push it
   down until it is partly submerged. Hypothesize, observe, and
   discuss.
3. Place a glass tumbler in an aquarium so that the glass will fill
   with water. Then, turn it upside down and lift until it is partly
   out of the water. Insert a rubber tube above the water line
   inside the glass. The tube must be of sufficient length to allow
   the demonstrator to blow air into the tube from the other end.
   Hypothesize, observe, and discuss.
4. Lower a glass tumbler, mouth downward, into an aquarium.
   With the other hand, lower another glass into the aquarium,
   letting it fill with water by tilting its mouth upward. Now, hold
   the second glass, mouth downward, above the first glass. Slowly
   tilt the first glass to let the air escape slowly, thus filling the
   second glass with air from the first. What does this show about
   air?
5. Seal a small-mouthed funnel tightly into the neck of a bottle
   with modeling clay. Pour a cup of water into the funnel
   quickly. What happens? Pass a soda straw through the funnel
   into the bottle. What happens? Why?

(The teacher will need to guide the discussion with appropriate
questions so that the discovery of the concept will be made.)

Timing and Organization: The entire class will be involved in making
observations of the demonstrations and discussing the results and
implications. This should take about 30 minutes.

Materials: Several balloons, 2 glass tumblers, 1 pan of water, 1
aquarium, 1 rubber tube about two feet long, 1 bottle, 1 funnel

with a relatively small throat, modeling clay, and several soda straws.

Evaluation: To be done the next day.

THURSDAY—FIRST WEEK

Objective: To evaluate the degree of understanding obtained during yesterday's lesson and to reinforce the concept.

Elements of Creative Behavior:

1. Elaboration (#5)

Activities: The students will be asked to restate the concept discussed yesterday. Then, the appropriate frames of the filmstrip *Physical Characteristics of Air* will be shown. Discussion will relate the filmstrip to the demonstration and will attempt to elaborate on the basic concept.

Timing and Organization: The evaluation should take about five minutes. The filmstrip and related discussion should require about 25 minutes and involve the entire class.

Materials: *Physical Characteristics of Air* from Jam Handy, 1 35mm filmstrip projector, and 1 screen.

Evaluation: The teacher will emphasize the parts of the filmstrip that reinforce the understandings which were found to be unclear during the initial evaluation period.

FRIDAY—FIRST WEEK

Objective: To lead the students to understand that air has weight.

Elements of Creative Behavior:

1. Experimenting with and Testing Ideas and Hunches (#7)
2. Learning from Failure (#8)

Activities: The teacher will conduct two demonstrations using students (when appropriate) while asking questions.

1. Hypothesize what will happen when you: deflate a basketball. Weigh it on a balance scale or other sensitive scale. Now reinflate the ball. Weigh it again. Compare the results.
2. Tie two inflated balloons at either end of a balance stick. Prick the neck of one of the balloons. Does the stick remain balanced? Explain.

(Appropriate frames of the filmstrip *Physical Characteristics of Air* will be shown. Discussion will relate this to the demonstrations).

Timing and Organization: The teacher will have several students assist in conducting the demonstrations. This will be an entire class activity, the discussion taking about 20 minutes. Another 10 minutes should be spent on the filmstrip.

Materials 1 basketball or other pneumatic ball, 1 balance scale, 2 balloons plus some extras, string or twine, balance stick or stiff wire, filmstrip: *Physical Characteristics of Air* from Jam Handy, 1 35mm projector, and 1 screen.

Evaluation: The teacher will observe the responses of the students to the discussion questions.

MONDAY AND TUESDAY—SECOND WEEK

Objective: To lead the students to understand that air exerts pressure in all directions.

Elements of Creative Behavior:

1. Experimenting with and Testing Ideas and Hunches (#7)
2. Learning from Failure (#8)

Activities: The teacher will direct students in ten demonstrations while leading a discussion and asking appropriate questions. Before each of the following experiments, students will hypothesize what will happen.

1. Place the tip of a medicine dropper under the surface of the water. Squeeze the dropper bulb. Release the bulb and let it swell up again. What happens? Explain.

2. Take some air out of an inflated paper bag by sucking. What happens? Why?

3. Remove the rubber tip from an eye dropper. Squeeze the air out of it. Push the open end firmly against the back of your hand. Observe. Explain.

4. Push a glass tumbler right side up to the bottom of a large container of water. (The water depth must be greater than the height of the glass). Turn the glass over under the water so that it is bottom-side up. Carefully, raise the glass full of water part way above the level of the water in the pan. Keep the rim of the glass below the surface of the water. Observe. What happens? Why? Explain.

5. Fill a glass with water. Press a filing card firmly against the rim of the glass. Hold the card in place while the glass is being

turned upside down. Explain why this is possible without spilling the water. Now, turn the glass on its side. Turn it again. What are the results? Why?

6. Select a bottle with a neck through which a hard boiled egg will not fit. Wad up a bit of paper, set it on fire, and drop it into the bottle. Quickly place the shelled egg, pointed end down, in the mouth of the bottle. Observe. Explain.

7. To get the egg out, turn the bottle upside down. Let the egg rest against the neck of the bottle, pointed end down. Now blow hard into the neck of the bottle and observe the results. Explain.

8. Select a tall glass or bottle. Wad up a little piece of paper, set it afire, and drop it into the bottle. Quickly stretch a rubber balloon over the mouth of the bottle. Explain what happens.

9. Fill a bottle with water except for a small bubble of air and replace the stopper. Turn the bottle on its side and try to make the bubble disappear by pressing the cork. Can it be done? Why? Why not?

10. Wet the bottom of a plumber's force cup and press it against a flat object. Lift the object with the force cup. Why is this impossible?

11. Put your finger over the top of a straw filled with water. Lift it. Tilt it. Take away your finger. What happens in each case? Why?

(Appropriate frames of the filmstrip *Physical Characteristics of Air* will be shown. Discussion will relate this to the experiments. Students will also be exposed to the reading center where appropriate reference materials will be available.)

Timing and Organization: Students will work in groups doing the experiments, allowing for as many to be done as possible. These activities should take about 20 minutes of each day. Another 10 minutes each day should be spent on related frames of the filmstrip or in reading related reference materials.

Materials: Medicine dropper, pan of water, large container of water, paper bag, glass tumbler, filing card(s), quart milk bottle, hard boiled egg with shell removed, tall glass or soda bottle, bottle with cork or rubber stopper, plumber's force cup (plumber's helper), soda straw(s), filmstrip: *Physical Characteristics of Air*, 1 35mm projector, 1 screen, and appropriate reference materials.

Evaluation: The teacher will observe the responses of the students to the experiments. Each should provide more insight and better understanding of the concept. The teacher must guide the students to appropriate reading assignments.

WEDNESDAY AND THURSDAY–SECOND WEEK

Objective: To lead the students to understand that air expands when it is heated and contracts when it is cooled.
Elements of Creative Behavior:
   1. Experimenting with and Testing Ideas and Hunches (#7)
   2. Learning from Failure (#8)
Activities: Teacher-directed demonstrations.
   1. Put a balloon over the mouth of a bottle. Place the bottle in a pan of hot water. Hypothesize what will happen. Observe. What happened? Now place the bottle in a pan of cold water or in a pan of crushed ice. Observe. Explain. Then place the bottle in the direct sunshine for a length of time. Observe periodically. Explain what happens. Then place the bottle in the shade. Observe periodically and explain the results.
   2. Put one cup of water in a can. Heat the water to a boil. Then replace the cap on the can. Immediately remove the can from the heat. Rub ice cubes along the sides of the can. Hypothesize the results. Observe carefully and explain. Replace the can on the burner and reheat. Again observe carefully. Remove the cap when reheated. Explain the results.
   3. Fill a bottle partly full of water. Place a cork or rubber stopper in the mouth of the bottle. Heat the bottle slowly. Hypothesize the results. Observe carefully. What happens? Why?
   4. Fill a bottle with hot water. Allow it to stand a few minutes until the bottle is warm. Now empty it and place the neck into a pan of water. Keep the opening submerged. Cool the bottle with crushed ice in a plastic bag. Hypothesize the results. Observe carefully. Explain.
(Note: This illustrates two concepts and should challenge the students.)
Timing and Organization: Selected students will assist the teacher in conducting the demonstrations. When necessary or appropriate, a demonstration may be repeated to increase the understanding.

After about 20 minutes the filmstrip and reading materials should be used to reinforce the learning.

Materials: Bottle, balloon, crushed ice in a plastic bag or ice cubes, pan of cold water, pan of hot water, hot plate or heating device, can with airtight cap, filmstrip: *Physical Characteristics of Air*, 1 35mm projector, 1 screen, and reading reference materials.

Evaluation: The teacher observes the responses of the students and evaluates their comments and further questions, then repeats the appropriate demonstrations and directs students to related reading and the filmstrip.

FRIDAY—SECOND WEEK

Objective: To review each concept and relate the concepts to each other.

Elements of Creative Behavior:

1. None today.

Activities: The film *Air and What it Does* will be shown. A discussion will be held on the film and other previous activities. The film may be shown again on the following day if deemed necessary or beneficial.

Timing and Organization: The film will take 11 minutes. The entire class will participate in the discussion for the remaining 19 minutes.

Materials: Film: *Air and What it Does* from Encyclopedia Britannica Films, 1 16mm sound projector, and 1 screen.

Evaluation: Teacher evaluation during the discussion period. Students should write up at least two experiments they have done and discuss the concepts illustrated through the activities.

MONDAY—THIRD WEEK

Objective: To relate the concepts studied to their usefulness to mankind.

Elements of Creative Behavior:

1. None today.

Activities: A brief discussion will be held to introduce the idea that air is useful to man as it pertains to the concepts studied. This will be followed by the film *The Air Around Us* and a discussion on the film.

Timing and Organization: Entire class activity. The introductory discussion will take about 5 minutes, the film 11 minutes, and the succeeding discussion about 15 minutes.

Materials: Film: *The Air Around Us* from Encyclopedia Britannica Films, 1 16mm projector, and 1 screen.

Evaluation: Teacher observation of student understandings.

TUESDAY–THIRD WEEK

Objective: To give students the opportunity to discover additional uses for the forces which air can provide.

Elements of Creative Behavior:

1. None today.

Activities: The students will read appropriate materials and references. The film *Experimenting with Air* will be shown.

Timing and Organization: The students should be involved with the reading for about 15 minutes. Then the film will last another 13 minutes.

Materials: Reference and related reading materials, film: *Experimenting with Air* from International Film Bureau, 1 16mm projector, and 1 screen.

Evaluation: To be done the next day.

WEDNESDAY–THIRD WEEK

Objective: To determine whether the behavioral objectives were achieved by the students.

Elements of Creative Behavior:

1. Fluency (#2)

Activities: The students will be asked to share information from their reading. The teacher will guide the discussion which will concentrate on the data from yesterday's film and reading. Students will brainstorm as many incidents as possible which serve to substantiate the concepts which have been studied.

Timing and Organization: The class will work together for the entire 30 minutes.

Materials: Reference materials as necessary.

Evaluation: Teacher observation of students' contributions.

THURSDAY–THIRD WEEK

Objective: To determine whether the behavioral objectives were achieved by the students.
Elements of Creative Behavior:
  1. None today.
Activities: Evaluation exercise which will measure the extent to which the stated objectives have been attained.
Timing and Organization: Following a 5 minute preparation period, the test will take 25 minutes.
Materials: Tests, extra pencils, and erasers.

FRIDAY–THIRD WEEK

Objective: To discuss the evaluation exercise and conduct further verbal evaluation.
Elements of Creative Behavior:
  1. Learning from Failure (#8)
Activities: A discussion will center on clarification of erroneous information.
Timing and Organization: The entire class will work together for the entire period.
Materials: Evaluation devices and/or questions selected by the teacher or students.
Evaluation: From the information received from the students during the discussion, the teacher will determine whether the stated behavioral objectives were met and the concepts understood.

APPENDIX D

WRITING FICTION (Elementary)

I. LONG-RANGE PURPOSES

    A. To extend ability of students to write fiction.
    B. To promote self-initiated writing.
    C. To encourage creativity.

II. CONCEPTS

    A. Activities which provide opportunities to become aware of the potentially "unusual" in a person's surroundings promote originality.
    B. A person can call ideas out of memory storage and expand upon them to recapture a past mood or to create a new one from a past experience.
    C. Activities which permit pupils to add to a stimulus in order to come up with a finished product develops elaboration.
    D. A fable is one creative method of illustrating an explicit general point.
    E. A fable has a specific structure of organization.
    F. Public sharing of written work is part of the creative process.
    G. In sifting stories to identify those that can be fairly readily acted out, pupils will learn about various fictional techniques in a very pragmatic, intuitive way.

III. ELEMENTS OF CREATIVE BEHAVIOR

    A. Fluency (#2)
    B. Imagination (#13)
    C. Synetics (#14)
    D. Elaboration (#5)
    E. Resourcefulness (#10)
    F. Originality (#4)

IV. BEHAVIORAL OBJECTIVES

(Learning Concept A)

A. The student will create a story by placing himself in the scene of a picture.

(Learning Concept B)

A. The student will recreate a mood based upon an especially memorable moment or scene from a book, play, or movie.

(Learning Concept C)

A. The student will be able to expand upon an unfinished sentence to create a story.

(Learning Concept D and E)

A. The student will be able to show knowledge of the structure of the fable by writing one.

B. The student will be able to illustrate an explicit general point by writing a fable.

(Learning Concept F)

A. The student will be able to share his written work in both small and large groups.

(Learning Concept G)

A. The student will be able to choose a paper suitable for dramatization (in small group work.)

V. EVALUATION

If the students are able to attain these instructional objectives successfully, the teacher can safely assume that they understand the concepts as stated. If not, the teacher must stop at whichever point the students have failed to understand and attempt either a revised procedure to achieve the same objectives or revised procedures to reach revised objectives.

PART 2

DAILY PLANS

DAY 1

Objective: To make up a story by placing himself in a scene, depicted in a magazine advertisement, of a camel standing in a New York City street.

Elements of Creative Behavior:

1. Fluency (#2)
2. Imagination (#13)
3. Originality (#4)

Activities:

1. Teacher displays the picture to the class. Give each child time to come up and study it for a few minutes.
2. Discuss the picture.
   a. What are these people saying to each other?
   b. What is this person doing or thinking?
   c. What might happen in this place?
3. Teacher asks each class member to place themselves in the scene. Discuss.
   a. What is happening now?
   b. What are you doing in the picture?
4. Students begin thinking up a story about the picture with themselves in it.
5. Students begin writing—may also dictate into a recorder or to the teacher.

Timing and Organization: Display of the picture and discussion should take about 30 minutes. Composing and dictating should take between 30-45 minutes. Longer time may be allowed if needed.

Materials: Key picture stimulus, pencils, paper, and a tape recorder for students who desire to dictate.

Evaluation: Production of a finished story, originality, pride, and enthusiasm.

DAY 2

Objective: To allow students to share stories.

Element of Creative Behavior:
1. None today.

Activities:
1. Students who volunteer, may read their stories to the entire class.
2. Divide class into trios and allow students to read stories to each other.

Timing and Organization: Students sharing stories with entire group will take about 15 minutes. Students working in trios for about 10 minutes.

Materials: Stories written on Day 1.

Evaluation: Based on number of students willing to read their stories to other classmates.

DAY 3

Objective: Each child will recreate in his own words an especially memorable scene or moment (small span of action) from a book, play, or movie without looking back at the original text.

Elements of Creative Behavior:
1. Synectics (#14)
2. Imagination (#13)
3. Elaboration (#5)

Activities:
1. Teacher relates to the class a scene from a book, play, or movie which was especially memorable to her.
2. Discussion with class of scenes that may have aroused a strong feeling in them.
3. Discuss what would happen if "you" were actually in that scene of the book, play, or movie.
4. Students are directed to write the scene by putting themselves back into it, becoming a part of it, perhaps taking the role of a character in it, making it happen again.
5. Students write or dictate into a recorder.

Timing and Organization: Discussion before writing may take 30-45 minutes. Then a break before composing. Composing may take 30-60 minutes.

Materials: Pencils, paper, memory, and imagination!

Evaluation: Production of a finished product. Pride, enthusiasm, creation of a mood in the story.

DAY 4

Objectives:
1. To dramatize a story chosen from the small group situation.
2. To discover, during discussion of papers in preparation for acting them out, which stories lend themselves to dramatization and why or why not.

Elements of Creative Behavior:
1. Resourcefulness (#10)
2. Originality (#4)
3. Imagination (#13)

Activities:
1. Class breaks up into small groups for purpose of choosing one paper to dramatize. Each group has three people, from the three grouped on Day 2.
2. In sifting stories for those that can be fairly readily acted out, pupils will learn that some stories cannot be acted out. They should come to some conclusions about why this is so.
   a. Too much description?
   b. Too indirect a relaying of the character's inner life?
   c. Too much commentary by the author?
   d. Do some stories have to be read and only read?
3. Students choose one paper and practice their dramatizations for 30 minutes.
4. Each group performs their dramatization.

Timing and Organization: Group reading and selection of paper should take 30 minutes. Practice should be about 30 minutes. Total presentation time for all plays will be 30-60 minutes. Teacher allows breaks between each of these three distinct steps.

Materials: Each student's finished paper from Day 3, extra space for practice and group work (hall, vacant room, etc.)

Evaluation: Did each group verbalize among themselves conclusions about the "playability" of the paper? Did the play they chose to do show some insight into those conclusions? Were they enthusiastic?

DAY 5

Objective: Each student will be able to write a complete story when given an unfinished sentence as a starter.

Elements of Creative Behavior:
1. Elaboration (#5)
2. Originality (#4)
3. Imagination (#13)

Activities:
1. Teacher gives an unfinished sentence such as, "Toby had been walking over the hill when _____ ."
2. The class discusses the possible story plots from this beginning.
3. Teacher then gives them an unfinished sentence for each of them to write a story of their own.
4. Students begin with "Nobody knew where it came from, but there it was, a big red_____ ." They finish the story.

Timing and Organization: Discussion should take 30 minutes. Writing should take 30-60 minutes.

Evaluation: Based on completion, originality, enthusiasm, pride.

DAY 6

Objective: To allow students to share stories.

Elements of Creative Behavior:
1. None today.

Activities:
1. Students who volunteer, may read their stories to the entire class.
2. Divide class into trios and allow students to read stories to each other.

Timing and Organization: Students sharing stories with entire group will take about 15 minutes. Students working in trios for about 10 minutes.

Materials: Stories written on Day 5.

Evaluation: Based on number of students willing to read their stories to other classmates.

DAY 7

Objective: To introduce children to the form and fun of fables.

Elements of Creative Behavior:
1. Fluency (#2)
2. Originality (#4)
3. Elaboration (#5)
4. Imagination (#13)

Activities:
1. Teacher reads the fable, "The Fox and the Grapes" from Aesop.
2. Discuss.
   a. What is a fable?
   b. What are the qualities of fables? (list on board)
   c. What is a moral? (list a few on the board)
   d. What part does the moral play in the fable?
3. Compose a fable as a class. Write the fable on the board.
4. Evaluate the class fable as a large group.
   a. Does it have all the listed characteristics of a fable?
   b. What is the moral of the class fable?
   c. Does the fable illustrate the moral?
   d. Do the characters fit the qualities in a fable?

Timing and Organization: Presentation of fable by the teacher should take 5-10 minutes. Discussion of fables, listing of characteristics needs about 30 minutes. Composition of class fable needs 30 minutes. Class evaluation about 20 minutes.

Materials: Copy of Aesop's Fables, and chalk.

Evaluation: Based on participation, enthusiasm, signs of enjoyment, insights about fables which were developed.

DAY 8

Objective: To write a fable and share it with other class members.

Elements of Creative Behavior:
1. Originality (#4)
2. Imagination (#13)
3. Elaboration (#5)

Activities:
1. Teacher reads another fable to the class, "The Grasshopper and the Ant" or "John J. Plenty" and "Fiddler Dan" by John Ciardi.
2. Class reviews characteristics of fables and rereads class fable from Day 7.

3. Each member composes his own fable (may do more than 1), remembering to incorporate the qualities of a fable.
4. Class divides into small groups to share fables.
5. Class may wish to share fables as one large group if activity 4 is successful and students wish.
6. Class may illustrate their fables.

Timing and Organization: Teacher presentation, discussion, and review will take 30 minutes. Composition will take 30-45 minutes. Small group sharing will take 15 minutes. Large group sharing may take 30-60 minutes. This lesson could extend to two days if large group work is desired.

Materials: Copy of "Aesop's Fables," "John J. Plenty" and "Fiddler Dan" by John Ciardi, pencils, paper, crayons, art paper, etc.

Evaluation: Completion, enthusiasm, small group participation, enjoyment, originality, each fable having the qualities of a fable.

APPENDIX E

INTERMEDIATE MATH—GEOMETRY (Secondary)

PART 1

LONG-RANGE PLANS

I. LONG-RANGE PURPOSES

    A. To introduce the study of polygons.

    B. To develop an understanding of the structure of geometric systems.

    C. To perform creative thinking processes in application of geometric algorithms.

II. LEARNING CONCEPTS

    A. The geometric shapes (triangle, rectangle, and square) have a specific number of sides and angles.

    B. Perimeter of a polygon is determined by the sum of the length of the sides.

    C. Area of a rectangle is equal to the length $\times$ the height.

    D. Because right triangles are halves of rectangles, their area is $1/2$ base $\times$ height.

    E. The area algorithm $1/2$ bh also applies to isosceles right triangles, which are halves of squares.

    F. Many polygons can be divided into right triangles in order to find their area.

III. ELEMENTS OF CREATIVE BEHAVIOR

    A. Synergy (#12)

    B. Experimenting with and Testing Ideas and Hunches (#7)

    C. Imagination (#13)

    D. Originality (#4)

    E. Synectics (#14)

    F. Flexibility (#3)

    G. Tolerance for Ambiguity (#9)

    H. Development of Humor (#1)

IV. BEHAVIORAL OBJECTIVES

(Learning Concept A)

A. Given a set of 12 drawings representing geometric shapes, the student will correctly identify triangles, rectangles, and squares.

B. Given a set of ten closed geometric shapes, the student will correctly record the number of sides and angles in at least eight of the figures.

C. Given a set of five drawings representing geometric shapes, the student will circle the right angles contained within them.

(Learning Concept B)

A. Given a set of concrete objects, the student will measure and record their perimeter to the nearest cm by adding the lengths of the sides.

© Kendall/Hunt Publishing Company

Acute Triangle

(Learning Concept C)

A. The student will construct at least five rectangles on the geoboard and correctly determine the area of each.

(Learning Concept D)

A. The student will demonstrate on the geoboard that right triangles are halves of rectangles by constructing five examples.

B. The student will demonstrate understanding of the 1/2 bh algorithm by correctly determining the area of right triangles.

(Learning Concept E)

A. The student will prove on the geoboard that the right triangle algorithm also applies to isosceles right triangles.

(Learning Concept F)

A. The student will employ creative problem solving by using knowledge concerning right triangles to determine the area of five unfamiliar polygons.

V. EVALUATION

If the students are able to complete these objectives successfully, the teacher can assume the concepts are understood. Since evaluation is a part of each day's activities, the unit can be restructured as needed.

PART 2

DAILY PLANS

MONDAY—FIRST WEEK

Objectives:
1. To introduce and define the following concepts: triangle, rectangle, square.
2. To have students find concrete examples of triangles, rectangles, and squares.

Elements of Creative Behavior:
1. Experimenting with and Testing Ideas and Hunches (#7)

Activities:
1. Using the "Creature Card" approach, give students an opportunity to generalize the attributes of △,◻,□.
2. Students are to locate and draw objects in the room shaped like △,◻,□.
3. In groups of three, students solve tangram puzzles using tagboard cutouts (△ and ◻).

Timing and Organization: The discussion of △, ◻ , and □ characteristics will involve all students for about ten minutes. Working independently drawing geometric objects of each shape will consume 30 minutes, after which the tangram activity will require at least 20 minutes.

Materials: Overhead projector, transparencies of shapes, paper, crayons, and tagboard tangrams.

Evaluation: Student identifies the three shapes discussed.

TUESDAY—FIRST WEEK

Objective: To introduce or review the concepts of *side* and *angle* in open and closed figures.

Elements of Creative Behavior:
1. Imagination (#13)
2. Originality (#4)

Activities:
1. Teacher introduces concepts in guided discovery method, giving clues and examples leading to student generalization.

2. Play "Guess My Rule" game with class, using polygons instead of numbers.

3. Challenge students to draw interesting and unusual figures with specified sides and angles, in open and closed figures.

Timing and Organization: Only ten minutes will be needed for class to understand, verbalize, and illustrate concepts *side* and *angle*. The "Guess My Rule" game can last enthusiastically for 20 minutes. Drawing of figures will be done in 25 minutes. Evaluation, five minutes.

Materials: Chalkboard and chalk, "Guess My Rule" machine or box, paper and pencil.

Evaluation: Teacher observation.

WEDNESDAY–FIRST WEEK

Objectives:
1. To introduce right angles.
2. To develop the concept of right angles in polygons.

Elements of Creative Behavior:
1. Flexibility (#3)
2. Originality (#4)
3. Synectics (#14)

Activities:
1. Teacher presents attributes of right angles and "not-right" angles; students find concrete examples by observation of the outside environment. (How many different examples can you find?)

2. Students create shapes on geoboard to meet specifications (game-style).

3. Students stand up and pretend they are the hands of a clock, simulating rays and determine the relationship of various times to right angles (larger, smaller, equal to right angle).

4. Students count triangles, rectangles, squares, and right angles in puzzle:

Timing and Organization: Introduction of concept and location of concrete examples, 15 minutes. The geoboard game as a class activity is done in 15 minutes. The clock activity requires about 15 minutes. Allow 15 minutes for students to become stumped and frustrated but challenged with the puzzle!

Materials: Chalkboard and chalk, realia, and dittoed puzzle handout.

Evaluation: Teacher observation of clock and geometry puzzle activities.

THURSDAY—FIRST WEEK

Objectives:
  1. To introduce concept *perimeter.*
  2. To motivate students to develop and practice using perimeter algorithm.

Elements of Creative Behavior:
  1. Tolerance for Ambiguity (#9)
  2. Imagination (#13)
  3. Originality (#4)

© Kendall/Hunt Publishing Company

"gee—ometry!"

Activities:
  1. Through use of the inquiry method, teacher leads students to discover meaning of word "perimeter" by looking at other words with same roots "peri" and "meter." From the new words generated, students generalize process of "around" and "measure."
  2. Students will measure two-dimensional polygons with metric rulers, employing problem solving processes and their own creative methods.

3. Students measure concrete objects such as perimeter of desk, globe, waist, school yard. . . .

Timing and Organization: Definition of word according to Latin roots and subsequent generalization as to meaning will last 25 minutes. Twenty minutes for individual measurement of two-dimensional objects. Group projects measuring larger concrete objects for fifteen minutes.

Materials: Dictionaries, metric rulers, string, tagboard polygons, tape measures, chalkboard, and chalk.

Evaluation: Teacher observation of students' perimeter-finding methods.

FRIDAY—FIRST WEEK

Objectives:
1. To introduce the concept of area as interior, occupied space.
2. To establish understanding that area units may vary.

Elements of Creative Behavior:
1. None today.

Activities:
1. With geoboards and teacher guidance, students construct rectangles and determine square units contained within them.
2. Students make charts together showing area, length, and height of many rectangles; discuss relationship, write algorithm.
3. Students find areas of two-dimensional concrete objects.
4. With Cuisenaire rods, students explore idea of variable units and play Cuisenaire Area game.

Timing and Organization: The topic introduction and geoboard activities should require approximately fifteen minutes. Finding the areas of concrete objects is an individual fifteen minute project. The Cuisenaire exploration/discovery will be 30 minutes.

Materials: Geoboards, rubberbands, chart paper and pens, metric rulers, Cuisenaire rods and dies.

Evaluation: Students construct five rectangles on the geoboard and explain how the area can be determined.

MONDAY—SECOND WEEK

Objectives:
1. To review area of rectangles.

2. To introduce right triangles.

3. To develop concept of right triangles as halves of $\square$.

Elements of Creative Behavior:

1. Imagination (#13)

2. Originality (#4)

Activities:

1. Using geoboards, students practice making rectangles and finding area.

2. Teacher reviews right angle characteristics, students construct and discover right $\triangleright$ within $\square$.

3. Students explore the relationship between $\square$ and $\triangleright$, charting results.

4. Groups of students make tangrams on geoboards which other students solve using only $\square$ and $\triangleright$.

5. Students make pictures on geoboards using only $\square$ and $\triangleright$, which tell a story and present to whole class.

Timing and Organization: Ten minutes is sufficient for the rectangle review. Introduction of the new concept requires five minutes. The charting of areas and relationships may take fifteen minutes. Tangram and story activities are flexible and some can take place in the first thirty minutes.

Materials: Geoboards and rubberbands (colorful), and chart paper.

Evaluation: Teacher observation.

TUESDAY–SECOND WEEK

Objectives:

1. To develop the algorithm, area = 1/2 bh.

2. To practice applying the algorithm.

3. To encourage logical inquiry.

Elements of Creative Behavior:

1. Experimenting with and Testing Ideas and Hunches (#7)

Activities:

1. Students use geoboards to develop area algorithm $\triangleright$.

2. Students are given dittoed practice sheets to practice finding area of $\triangleright$ in square centimeters.

3. Students determine area of tagboard right $\triangleright$ and arrange pieces into a $\square$, correlation between areas of $\triangleright$ and $\square$ derived by utilizing the tagboard area puzzle.

Timing and Organization: Only about 10 minutes are required for students to develop the algorithm which they will practice using for the next 20 minutes. The tagboard area puzzle, a small group activity, involves approximately 30 minutes.

Materials: Geoboards and rubberbands, dittoed practice sheets, pencils, metric rulers, tagboard, and right triangle/rectangle puzzles.

Evaluation: Teacher observation.

WEDNESDAY–SECOND WEEK

Objectives:
1. To provide situations for students to strengthen area-finding skills.
2. To develop in students problem-solving strategies.

Elements of Creative Behavior:
1. Experimenting with and Testing Ideas and Hunches (#7)
2. Imagination (#13)

Activities:
1. Small groups of students play the Geo-Area game.
2. Individual students solve the Polygonville Right Triangle Factory Problem by seeing if they can use the paper most efficiently.

Timing and Organization: Thirty minutes of playing the Geo-Area game will prepare the students to spend half an hour on the Polygonville problem.

Materials: Geoboards and rubberbands, Geo-Area cards, paper, scissors, metric rulers, and Polygonville Right Triangle Factory Problem.

Evaluation: Teacher observation.

THURSDAY–SECOND WEEK

Objective: To introduce isosceles right triangles.

Elements of Creative Behavior:
1. Originality (#4)
2. Imagination (#13)

Activities:
1. Students will look at examples of isosceles right triangles and deduce the meaning of words "isosceles."

2. Students will prove on the geoboard that the $\triangle$ area algorithm applies to isosceles right $\triangle$ in an individual conference with the teacher.

3. Students will practice creative writing with a geometry theme.

Timing and Organization: After working for 10-15 minutes with the isosceles concept, students will spend the next 40 minutes enjoying creative writing while the teacher confers with individuals.

Materials: Geoboards and rubberbands, chalkboard and chalk, pencil, paper, crayons, and paints.

Evaluation: Individual conferences discussing creative writing efforts.

FRIDAY—SECOND WEEK

Objectives:
1. To provide application of area algorithm.
2. To develop higher-level thinking strategies by using principles of geometry in problem solving.

Elements of Creative Behavior:
1. Development of Humor (#1)

Activities:
1. The students will each find the area of five unfamiliar polygons, all of which can be divided into right triangles. Punning exercises involving geometry principles will be used for "warm-up."

Timing and Organization: The activity will take most students 30-45 minutes. Those finishing will be urged to create some geometry puns.

Materials: Dittoed worksheets of unfamiliar polygons, pencils, and metric rulers.

Evaluation: Teacher will check the worksheets. If students need additional help, they should be worked with individually.

MONDAY-TUESDAY—THIRD WEEK

Objectives: To construct collages and/or a mural using the geometric shapes and sizes.

Elements of Creative Behavior:
1. Synergy (#12)

Activities:
1. Students will choose a mural planning committee which will

adapt a mural theme. Each student who so desires will have the opportunity to create a portion of the mural using one or more of the basic designs which have been studied.

2. Students will also construct collages individually, during the time they are not actively participating in construction of the mural.

Timing and Organization: The collage and mural construction will take two days.

Materials: Whatever needed for construction of murals and collages. These will vary according to the group and individuals.

Evaluation: Observation and student participation.

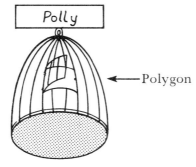

APPENDIX F

LANGUAGE EXPERIENCE APPROACH TO READING

LONG-RANGE PLANS

I. LONG-RANGE PURPOSES

A. To extend the ability of students to interpret the printed word in view of their individual background.
B. To use the language and ideas of children as a basis for skill development.
C. To encourage creativity.

II. CONCEPTS

A. A person's ideas are worthy of expression.
B. Activities which provide for interaction of children (sharing pictures and ideas, reading to children, storytelling, creative writing, and others) help to develop and expand reading skills.
C. Oral expression is stimulated through art activities.
D. Written expression flows from the oral expression.
E. Motivation occurs upon seeing one's own language in written form.
F. Students desire to read what they and their classmates have written.

III. ELEMENTS OF CREATIVE BEHAVIOR

A. Originality (#4)
B. Imagination (#13)
C. Problem Sensitivity (#11)
D. Elaboration (#5)

IV. BEHAVIORAL OBJECTIVES

(Learning Concept A)
A. The student will be able to verbalize his thoughts pertaining to art work he produces.

(Learning Concept B)

A. The student will create a story by sharing phrases or sentences.

B. The student will read what he has written to himself, other children, or to an adult.

C. The student will write either his own story or a story he has helped to create.

D. The student will be able to write a story about a picture he drew.

E. When writing his own story, the student will spell his words with 75 percent accuracy.

(Learning Concept C)

A. The student will request the opportunity to write stories after relating them verbally.

(Learning Concept D)

A. The student will do additional writing after receiving recognition of his written productions.

(Learning Concept E)

A. When granted free-time activities, the student will voluntarily read his work and that of his peers.

V. EVALUATION

If the students are able to successfully attain these instructional objectives, the teacher can safely assume that they understand the concepts as stated. If not, the teacher must retrace the planning-evaluation processes. Either the concepts were unattainable and/or the activities were not appropriate for the objectives developed.

PART 2

DAILY PLANS

MONDAY – FIRST WEEK

Objective: To encourage the telling of a fanciful tale; pretending to be something other than yourself.

Elements of Creative Behavior:

1. Problem Sensitivity (#11)
2. Originality (#4)
3. Imagination (#13)
4. Elaboration (#5)

Activities:

1. Listen to the stories entitled: *If I Were a Piano* or *If I Were a Basket of Flowers.*
2. Discuss.
3. Children then begin thinking of an imaginary story of their own.
4. Teacher then suggests some sample titles such as:
   a. a wild animal.
   b. a penny.
   c. an old car.
   d. a telephone.
   e. a bug.
5. Students dictate stories to teacher or teacher aide for recording.

Timing and Organization: The story will take ten minutes, and fifteen minutes should be allotted for the student to think of ideas. Dictation of stories takes 30 minutes.

Materials: Tape recorder for listening to sample stories, half-ruled paper, crayons, and pencils.

Evaluation: Based on participation, degree of interest, and imagination.

TUESDAY – FIRST WEEK

Objective: To determine what makes a creative, interesting story.

Elements of Creative Behavior:

1. Problem Sensitivity (#11)
2. Originality (#4)

3. Imagination (#13)

4. Elaboration (#5)

Activities:

1. React to some of Monday's stories and discuss what makes them interesting and creative.

2. Students draw a picture of their own and write a story telling what it is about.

Timing and Organization: Discussion of stories for 20 minutes. Story writing for 30 minutes.

Materials: Yesterday's picture stories, half-ruled paper, pencils, and crayons.

Evaluation: Based on creative ideas.

WEDNESDAY—FIRST WEEK

Objective: To introduce children to the fun of creating riddles.

Elements of Creative Behavior:

1. Problem Sensitivity (#11)

2. Originality (#4)

3. Imagination (#13)

4. Elaboration (#5)

Activities:

1. Place a surprise riddle on the board. (Sample: He has a funny face; he has funny, big shoes; he makes people laugh.)

2. Write the teacher's riddle.

3. Students then draw a picture illustrating the riddle. After discussing the pictures, have students tell a riddle to the rest of the class.

Timing and Organization: Five minutes to copy riddle. Allow 15 minutes to draw the picture and ten minutes to discuss them. Twenty minutes for students to share riddles they know with entire class.

Materials: Teacher's riddle, half-ruled paper, pencils, and crayons.

Evaluation: Determine whether students enjoyed working with riddles.

THURSDAY—FIRST WEEK

Objective: To write a riddle.

Elements of Creative Behavior:

1. Originality (#4)
2. Imagination (#13)
3. Elaboration (#5)

Activities:

1. Teacher suggests possible sources for riddles and reads one to the class.
2. Students draw a picture illustrating the solutions to the riddle.

Timing and Organization: Teacher input and story—15 minutes. Individual work for 30 minutes.

Materials: Half-ruled paper, pencils, crayons, books with riddles.

Evaluation: Creativity, interest and participation in the development of riddles.

FRIDAY—FIRST WEEK

Objective: To promote listening for humor.
Elements of Creative Behavior:

1. Originality (#4)
2. Imagination (#13)
3. Elaboration (#5)

Activities:

1. The teacher reads "Little Apple and the Long Black Pipe" from the *Anthology of Children's Literature* by Arbuthnot.
2. Students illustrate a part of the story they especially enjoyed.

Timing and Organization: Read "Little Apple . . ."—20 minutes. Drawing of a story part—20 minutes. Discussion of drawings—20 minutes.

Materials: *Anthology of Children's Literature* by Arbuthnot, half-ruled paper, and crayons.

Evaluation: Did illustrations show that students identified with Chinese culture?

TUESDAY—SECOND WEEK

Objective: To develop respect for many kinds of work and/or labor.
Elements of Creative Behavior:

1. Problem Sensitivity (#11)
2. Originality (#4)
3. Imagination (#13)
4. Elaboration (#5)

Activities:
  1. Introduce the concept of work.
  2. Students share their parents' occupations.
  3. Pantomine some skill involved in their work.
  4. Write a story telling what they do.
Timing and Organization: Students sharing stories with entire group—15 minutes. Students work in trios—10 minutes for first round. Change trios twice for two more periods of 10 minutes each.
Materials: Stories written on Tuesday.
Evaluation: Based on number of students willing to read their stories to other classmates.

THURSDAY—SECOND WEEK

Objective: To develop interest in home activities and promote sharing of ideas.
Elements of Creative Behavior:
  1. Problem Sensitivity (#11)
  2. Originality (#4)
  3. Imagination (#13)
  4. Elaboration (#5)
Activities:
  1. Draw a picture illustrating your favorite television program.
  2. Write a story about the picture.
  3. Share the stories.
Timing and Organization: Drawing pictures—15 minutes. Writing stories—15 minutes. Sharing stories—30 minutes. (Entire class participates in sharing exercise).
Materials: Half-ruled paper, crayons, and pencils.
Evaluation: Based on the interest in sharing about home activities and the fluency of ideas.

FRIDAY—SECOND WEEK

Objectives:
  1. To reinforce some of the things learned about zoo animals.
  2. To learn the difference between the zoo and the circus.
  3. To learn certain circus terms and animal names.

Elements of Creative Behavior:
1. Problem Sensitivity (#11)
2. Originality (#4)
3. Imagination (#13)
4. Elaboration (#5)

Activities:
1. Read poetry about circuses and discuss with class.
2. Draw a picture of a zoo or circus.
3. Write a story about the picture.
4. Share pictures.

Timing and Organization: Group discussion—10 minutes. Draw picture—15 minutes. Write a story—15 minutes. Sharing of pictures in trios (2 ten-minute round robins with different trio members)—20 minutes.

Materials: Poem about circuses, half-ruled paper, crayons, and pencils.

Evaluation: Through stories, pictures, and discussion, students should have distinguished between zoos and circuses. By the end of the two-week period, the teacher should have had ample opportunity to evaluate the attainment of the behavioral objectives. Normally at the lower elementary level in such a program, it will be unnecessary to devote a formal class period to this activity. The teacher should be continually referring to the stated behavioral objectives and evaluate them periodically.

APPENDIX G

CONTEMPORARY WORLD PROBLEMS (Secondary)

PART 1

LONG-RANGE PLANS

I. LONG-RANGE PURPOSES

A. To increase the awareness of the student as to the diversity and level of impact that moral/social questions present to society.

B. To enhance the development of research skills and increase the students' skills in material presentation in written and debate forms.

C. To encourage creative participation by all students.

II. LEARNING CONCEPTS

A. There are intense traditional values that people adhere to strongly when subjects like gun control are discussed.

B. America's gun control laws contain many loopholes which have not curtailed the availability of guns as originally intended.

C. To date, no licensing procedures for gun owners similar to automobile licensing regulations are in existence.

D. Because of certain gun control restrictions there is a large demand for black market guns which has created a very dangerous situation.

E. Pressure groups such as the National Rifle Association and some hunting clubs have exerted strong legislative pressures against gun control.

F. A basic area of controversy has been the interpretation of the U.S. constitutional guarantee which allows American citizens the right to bear arms.

G. The gun control controversy is a relatively new and extremely volatile topic of debate with intense support from both sides.

H. The gun control controversy touches on many interrelated philosophical questions.
I. There are different ways of organizing a group in order to achieve efficient division of labor and performance of duties.
J. There are fundamental skills to be used when formulating a position paper or presenting arguments in a debate.

III. ELEMENTS OF CREATIVE BEHAVIOR

A. Experimenting with and Testing Ideas and Hunches (#7)
B. Tolerance for Ambiguity (#9)
C. Resourcefulness (#10)
D. Problem Sensitivity (#11)

IV. BEHAVIORAL OBJECTIVES

(Learning Concept A)
1. The student will be able to read gun control propaganda (pro and con) published by special interest groups and analyze the rationale for the various positions taken.

(Learning Concept B)
1. The student will be able to research the gun control legislation and use the data to present arguments in both written and debate form.

(Learning Concept C)
1. The student will be able to utilize the research pertaining to gun licensing attempts in the actual debate in order to argue a given position.

(Learning Concept D, F, and G)
1. The student will be able to research the history of gun control legislation including material on (a) black market gun dangers; (b) recorded impacts of gun control legislation on population and social control; and (c) history of the efforts of both sides of the controversy.

(Learning Concept E)
1. The student will be able to express personal moral and/or value judgments for either the pro or the con side of the written and verbal arguments and presentations.

(Learning Concept H)
1. The student will be able to recognize and weed out the various indirectly-related philosophical questions and use only directly related material in presentations.

(Learning Concept I)
1. The student, through group work, will be able to assemble the research material into a position paper to be used in debate.

(Learning Concept J)
1. The student will be able to present either side of the question in debate.

V. EVALUATION

If the students successfully complete the objectives, the teacher should assume they understand the concepts and the long-range purpose has been accomplished. If the objectives were not performed adequately, the teacher should rework the planning sequences to see if the concepts were unattainable or the daily activities were not appropriate.

PART 2

DAILY PLANS

MONDAY–FIRST WEEK

Objectives:
1. To determine the personal opinion of the student on the issue of gun control.
2. To introduce the two-week assignment and explain the various stages as follows: group assignment and organization; research of the problem; outside speakers; presentations; group evaluation of material; group formulation of position paper; group debate.

Elements of Creative Behavior:
1. None

Activities:
1. The students will write a short essay stating their personal opinion and belief on the subject of gun control.
2. Introduction and discussion of the assignment and its various parts.

Timing and Organization: The students will be given the first 15 to 20 minutes of the class to write their individual opinion papers. The remainder of the period will be used to introduce and discuss the assignment and will involve the entire class.

Materials: paper, pens, chalkboard, and chalk.

Evaluation: The teacher decides if the students understand the assignment by the discussion and then categorizes the opinion papers into pro or con groups.

TUESDAY–FIRST WEEK

Objectives:
1. To form groups in accordance with students' personal wishes when possible.
2. To make the students aware of the different ways of organizing a group.
(i.e.: democratic leadership; absolute spokesperson; nonleader plurality; new or original structure)

Elements of Creative Behavior:
1. Experimenting with and Testing Ideas and Hunches (#7)
2. Tolerance for Ambiguity (#9)
3. Resourcefulness (#10)
4. Problem Sensitivity (#11)

Activities:
1. The students will be divided into groups according to their opinion and the teacher will explain the various ways to organize a group to function efficiently.
2. The groups will discuss and decide upon a group structure.
3. The groups will be assigned the research. A discussion pertaining to the research or available materials will take place.
4. The groups will divide the workload among the members.

Timing and Organization: For the first five to ten minutes of the class, the groups will be formed. In the next five to ten minutes there will be an explanation of the manner in which groups can be organized and the structure will be decided upon. For the remaining time, the various types of research will be discussed and group work will begin.

Materials: Paper, pens, chalkboard, and chalk.

Evaluation: The teacher, through discussion and observation, will decide if the various tasks are understood and completed.

WEDNESDAY—FIRST WEEK

Objectives:
1. To make the students aware of the available materials.
2. To begin the research.

Elements of Creative Behavior:
1. Resourcefulness (#10)

Activities:
1. Students will meet in the library and have a brief orientation to research procedures and location of materials.
2. Students begin the research.

Timing and Organization: The first ten to fifteen minutes will be utilized for instruction with discussions about available research material. The rest of the time will be used for research.

Materials: Paper, pens, and the library.

Evaluation: The teacher will make a personal evaluation of progress by observation.

THURSDAY—FIRST WEEK

Objectives:
1. To make the students aware of the basic debate skills.
2. Relate these skills to ways and means of research material collection.
3. Continue research.

Elements of Creative Behavior:
  1. Tolerance for Ambiguity (#9)
  2. Resourcefulness (#10)
  3. Problem Sensitivity (#11)
Activities:
  1. Hear a presentation of basic debate skills and strategies from the debate instructor of the school.
  2. Discuss how the skills should be applied to the materials collected.
  3. Continue research.
Timing and Organization: The entire class will listen to the debate instructor and then discuss skill application to research gathering. Whatever remains of the time will be used in research.
Materials: Paper, pens, and the library.
Evaluation: The teacher will make an evaluation as to the worth of the day's activities.

FRIDAY—FIRST WEEK

Objectives:
  1. Continue research.
Elements of Creative Behavior:
  1. Resourcefulness (#10)
Activities:
  1. Research in the library.
Timing and Organization: The entire period will be used for library research.
Materials: Paper, pens, and library.
Evaluation: Will be based on the effectiveness of the research tasks.

MONDAY-TUESDAY—SECOND WEEK

Objectives:
  1. To give the students an idea of how to present a good argument for one side of a question.
  2. To make the students aware of interest group information that is available.
Elements of Creative Behavior:
  1. Tolerance for Ambiguity (#9)
  2. Problem Sensitivity (#11)
Activities:
  1. A presentation of both interest group representatives (pro and con).

2. Inner-group discussion about the use of written and oral propaganda in their presentation (time permitting).

Timing and Organization: The guest speakers for each gun control position (pro and con) will have approximately 2/3 of the class time for a presentation and distribution of materials. The remainder of the time will be used for group discussions of the presentations.

Materials: Paper, pens, and written handouts.

Evaluation: Depending on effectiveness of the speaker and following discussion.

WEDNESDAY—SECOND WEEK

Objectives:
1. To make the students aware of what a position paper is.
2. To develop the position papers of each group in sufficient detail.

Elements of Creative Behavior:
1. Tolerance for Ambiguity (#9)
2. Problem Sensitivity (#11)

Activities:
1. A description of and discussion about a position paper.
2. Group work on formulation of position paper.

Timing and Organization: The first minor segment of the class time will be used for explanation and discussion of the written presentation paper. Whatever time remains will be used in group work on the paper.

Materials: Paper and pens.

Evaluation: The teacher will determine the extent of understanding and application of the material.

THURSDAY—SECOND WEEK

Objectives:
1. To finish the position paper as a group effort.
2. To introduce the groups to the opposite position by trading position papers.
3. Inform the groups of their responsibility to argue for the opposing opinion in the coming debate.

Elements of Creative Behavior:
1. Experimenting with and Testing Ideas and Hunches (#7)
2. Tolerance for Ambiguity (#9)
3. Resourcefulness (#10)

Activities:
1. The groups will complete the position papers.
2. The position papers will be switched and inner-group discussions of new position to be represented will ensue.

Timing and Organization: The first one-half of the class time will be used in group work on completion of the position papers. Two minutes will be allowed for switching the papers and informing the groups that they must present the opposite side. The remainder of the time will be used for inner-group strategy in connection with the new presentation.

Materials: Paper and pens.

Evaluation: The teacher will observe and evaluate the success of the paper formulations, acceptance of the new position, and the ability to adapt a new argument.

FRIDAY–SECOND WEEK

Objectives:
1. To debate the issue of gun control.

Elements of Creative Behavior:
1. Experimenting with and Testing Ideas and Hunches (#7)
2. Tolerance for Ambiguity (#9)
3. Resourcefulness (#10)
4. Problem Sensitivity (#11)

Activities:
1. The groups will put the final touches on their presentations.
2. Debate exercise.

Timing and Organization: The first five minutes will be used for group work on the presentations with the remaining time used for debate.

Materials: Position papers and knowledge acquired through research.

Evaluation: Through teacher observation of the composition and debate activity.

(Note: This plan was adapted from a plan created by Donald Higgins, a student at Eastern Washington State College.)